Love Being Human™

The Key to Harmony Within You

Dr. Vivian Carrasco

Copyright © 2023 Vivian Carrasco

All rights reserved. No part of this book may be reproduced by any mechanical, photographic, or electronic process, or in the form of a phonographic recording, nor may it be stored in a retrieval system, transmitted, or otherwise be copied for public or private use—other than for 'fair use' as brief quotations embodied in articles and reviews—without prior written permission of the publisher.

The information in this book is true and complete to the best of the author's knowledge. Any advice or recommendations are made without guarantee on the part of the author or publisher. The author and publisher disclaim any liability in connection with the use of this information.

Publisher's Cataloging-in-Publication data

Names: Carrasco, Vivian Hernandez, author.

Title: Love being human : the key to harmony within you / Vivian Hernandez Carrasco.

Description: Weatherford, TX: Wisdom Within, 2023.

Identifiers: LCCN: 2023911688 | ISBN: 979-8-9885249-1-5

Subjects: LCSH Self-actualization (Psychology) | Success--Psychological aspects. | Conduct of life. | Spirituality. | Self-help. | BISAC SELF-HELP / Meditations | SELF-HELP / Spiritual | BODY, MIND & SPIRIT / Inspiration & Personal Growth | BODY, MIND & SPIRIT / Healing / Prayer & Spiritual

Classification: LCC BF637.S8 .C37 2023 | DDC 646.7--dc23

Printed in the USA

Cover and Interior Design: Kelly Exeter

To my loving husband, David, for each step and every breath of our beautiful life together; to my sons, Joshua and Jacob, y'all are seriously the best parts of me.

In memory of my beloved Padrino, love you more.

Those who live passionately teach us how to love.
Those who love passionately teach us how to live.
~ Sarah Ban Breathnach

Contents

INTRODUCTION.................................... 1

    Love Being Human............................ 3

    Who am I?...................................... 7

    About this book............................... 8

    Before you begin............................. 12

SECTION 1 – LOVE 13

    What is love?................................. 17

    Moving toward what we love 21

    Accessing love 25

    Self-compassion 31

    Changing memories into love 35

    Meditations on love......................... 40

    Final reflection: Love....................... 56

SECTION 2 – BEING 57

    Start with your breath 64

    Release yourself from the "shoulds".............. 75

    A transformative change of heart 82

    The Texas Two-Step 89

Your soul knows where to go......................... 91

The power of igniting your imagination 114

Final reflection: Being 119

SECTION 3 - HUMAN 121

You're smarter than your thinking 127

Who are you beneath the chaos?.................. 130

Understanding yourself better.................... 135

Journey to joy.................................. 149

Your body knows................................. 160

You can't do this alone.......................... 164

The journey to self 166

Final reflection: Human 172

CONCLUSION....................................173

ACKNOWLEDGMENTS..............................177

ABOUT THE AUTHOR..............................179

Introduction

"How can I begin anything new with all of yesterday in me?"
~ Leonard Cohen

Is this really it?

What am I missing here?

Why aren't I happy?

For my whole life, I'd been an "achiever". And by the age of 35, I'd achieved and accomplished everything I'd ever wanted for my life–more than I ever imagined. So in return, I expected a feeling of completion. Of accomplishment. Of confidence. Of certainty.

But as I stood at that place in my life and looked around, I just felt sad. Which led to feelings of guilt.

Why can't I just be grateful for everything and let it be? Maybe I did it wrong. Maybe there's something else.

Ah, that's it. There must be something else.

So I resigned from my consulting job.

I went back to college and finished my doctorate.

I mothered my eldest through finishing high school and leaving home.

My husband retired from his job in the military, and we moved house.

And through it all the guilt and pain persisted.

Why aren't I happy?

Did I make the right decisions when I was climbing all those ladders?

Should I change direction again?

The uncertainty was killing me. I added self-medication (i.e., wine) to the medication I was already taking for anxiety and depression.

Why? To stop feeling anything.

On the surface I was a high-functioning individual, moving around the world with a smile on my face. But on the inside, an emotional tornado was tearing me apart. I was constantly torn between what I thought I should do and had always done, and something else. Except I didn't know what that "something else" was.

This unraveling went on for five years.

Finally, when I turned 40 in 2013, I decided to do something about my pain.

In October that year I went on a retreat.

Seventeen days of silence.

Nowhere to run.

No way to numb my thoughts.

I had to sit with them.

I had to sit in them.

That retreat opened the door for me to stop running away from what I feared and towards my own joy.

As I crossed the threshold into a new way of being, I was given a set of instructions to share with you.

Love Being Human

This is my version of timeless truth, built on wisdom from within and around the world. It translates into a promise and a process, both of which I'll share with you.

This is where you and I meet: In the yearning, in that seeking to witness what wants to happen through us, deepening the level of who we are and how we serve.

You're no longer moving away from what you fear. Instead, you're moving toward what you love and what brings you joy.

This book is born out of my personal journey. One where I went from being certain about my roles and my place in the world to standing at a threshold I had to cross; a doorway I had to step through to enable a new way of being.

Thanks to the transition and transformation I went through, my life today is very different from my life back then. You need to get what you *wanted* before you realize it's not what you *needed*. This shift represents a deepening within.

And that deepening gives you the meaning you were looking for.

It instills in you the sense of fulfillment and purpose you knew was there somewhere. It also gives back your confidence, along with a sense of direction.

That shift in your sense of direction is vital. Why? Because you're no longer moving away from what you fear. Instead, you're moving toward what you love and what brings you joy.

And that's a completely different way to travel through life.

You can find harmony within. Your thinking, feeling, and being can all align so everything moves in the same direction.

Your success is no longer what people see on the outside, even though you'll probably be just as (if not more) successful. Instead of being driven by ambition, you'll be pulled forward by aspiration. You'll find yourself grounded in a deeply rooted sense of Being. You'll be on a path you believe in. You'll make your own path, not just follow the leader or what you see being done. You'll know to the core of your being that it's what you need to do, and a way to give your best in the world.

You'll do work you're proud of. You won't be acquiring, getting, or fulfilling from outside to have more (or to fill that missing spot) because the meaning will be there.

Imagine moving with a clear sense of purpose. Imagine having a crystal-clear vision and a deep knowing of who you are and what you want in a life that's full of ease and joy, meaning, and purpose instead of that muddy, unclear "middle".

I now have a better relationship with myself. And it's deepened and clarified the relationships I have with others. I have a greater sense of freedom. The freedom "to do" rather than freedom "from." It's the freedom you've chosen to have a well-lived life and to create a better world for you and the people who matter most to you.

There's a way to improve the quality of your human journey from your head to your heart. But the journey involves letting go of your need for doing, fitting in, and looking for outward validation. Instead, you'll enjoy being, belonging, and awakening to the deep, simple, and mysterious world within.

To do that you'll need to become more curious, establish priorities aligned with your deepest values, and experience the energy, power, and inspiration that comes from the silence of your heart.

Who am I?

I'm a Master Certified Life Coach who's trained extensively in:

- expanding self-awareness
- the complexities of the human psyche
- the science and intelligence of the body
- universal spiritual wisdom traditions.

I also come from a lineage of Curanderas (indigenous mestizo healers for their community).

I've been teaching adults in group programs and workshops since 1997. Before developing the *Love Being Human* method, I conferred my doctoral degree, specializing in leadership development. I had a long and successful career working with businesses and industry, building local, regional, and national collaborative partnerships.

But success didn't make me happy.

It's now my mission to teach *Love Being Human* to help women create a beautiful, inspired life by giving them a vision, a process, and integrative practices to move from turmoil to a personal spiritual inner transformation.

About this book

Love Being Human is a simple three-step system that provides practical direction for moving through your transformation.

Each section of this book illustrates principles of *Love Being Human* I've applied and explored in my own life, with my clients, and in the group programs I lead.

It also includes practical tools you can use to calm your doubt and build your belief muscle by developing your own unique habits of the heart.

You'll see your own experience in a very special way—as a deep, lived experience.

You'll know the difference between what your mind *wants* and what your heart *needs*.

I'll explain how you can:

- interrupt negative mental patterns
- shift your mindset

- open your heart
- connect deeper.

I'll teach you specific techniques that will give you just enough space to center yourself and bring forward your next best choice.

Love Being Human is a system of integration. An infinite loop that starts and never stops. You can start at any point.

This book is divided into three sections.

SECTION I looks at *Love* as an interdependence—a connection and sharing of energy and information flow. You're not an individual living in your body, separate from the world and the people around you. Aligning your actions and intentions with the belief that you're interconnected shifts you from the trap of busyness to the depths of your true nature. You become deeply rooted in:

- belonging
- being more authentically creative
- being connected to yourself, others, and nature
- doing work you're proud of
- creating a future you want to see.

By understanding your design, and how you make decisions as a human, you can replace bad habits and negative mental patterns with something better.

SECTION 2 revolves around *Being*. It focuses on awakening through presence and prayer. Spirituality is unique to everyone, but in my experience we find ourselves drawn to a kinder and more relational sense of the sacred—a spiritual life rooted in love and belonging. In this space we explore the wonder and mystery of life, focusing on the sacred in everyday experiences. We awaken through a spiritual path/practice in our daily life. These experiences transform into spiritual practices because they cultivate awareness—an expanded awareness that shifts your relationship with your thoughts, allowing them to flow without being carried away.

SECTION 3 shows that to be *Human* you need to expand your understanding and awareness of your body. In this section, you'll learn how to notice, name and decipher the intellect in the emotions we feel. By understanding your design, and how you make decisions as a human, you can replace bad habits and negative mental patterns with something better. You'll move from competition and comparison to an awareness of what's best for you, drawn forward by your own inner wisdom.

Each section builds on the key skills and central principles of curiosity and exploring what's possible. The integrative practices are tools you can use now in your practical day-to-day life to move your knowledge from your head to your heart through your hands.

What I'm offering you is a roadmap–a path for you to take so you can love being human again by cultivating your inner joy and unique truth through a direct experience. This transformational process will help you achieve harmony within yourself, and between you and the people you love.

Before you begin

Give yourself permission to imagine.

Call yourself out if you mistakenly believe you know all the options, or that you need to figure it all out on your own.

Give yourself time, space, and a tiny bit of kindness for something else to show up.

Give yourself permission to imagine something different as your brain and heart set out on an adventure together.

Your awareness will naturally look for things that support your intention. You'll be moved in ways you won't even notice.

Waking up from our slumber is what we're made for–the work we need to do to become fully human.

Soul work is the great work.

May my story and these practices help you on your journey.

SECTION I

Love

"Your task is not to seek for love, but merely to seek and find all the barriers within yourself that you have built against it."

~ RUMI

Love

It's April 2014, and I'm walking down the street to where I'm meeting my husband, David, for dinner.

As I approach one of the intersections, there's a sudden shift in my being and awareness. It's as if all the lights have come on. Colors, sounds, and everything else become high definition. I shift my purse from my right side to my left, and sort of stand at attention.

At this particular intersection there are four lanes to cross. The little man turns white, and I begin to cross.

As I enter the third lane, I look to my left and see a yellow Mustang slowly coming forward. I remember making eye contact with the driver. I remember thinking the driver had seen me and was slowing down. But he hasn't, and as I'm crossing the lane his yellow Mustang hits me.

Somewhere between being hit by the car and landing in the middle of the intersection, something happens.

It's hard to describe. But I'll try.

I re-experienced *every interaction* I'd ever had that could be defined as love—every smile, every word, and every face. It was like someone had turned a crank handle, and all the love I'd ever generated in my entire life was being recalled.

All that love released something in me. Something in my cells. Something in my body. It cleansed me of all my pain and sorrow. Everything negative my body and soul had been holding onto fell like a curtain.

And when it fell, I was released.

That release felt like my spirit being knocked out of my body. And after it was knocked out of its "container", it spread over everything. "I" was everywhere. And there was this sense of serenity and pure peace.

I'm not sure how long I was "out"–blissed out in this state of pure peace. But at some point, I opened my eyes and saw a man standing over me.

"Are you okay?" he asked.

Incredibly, I *was* okay. I wasn't hurt, and I could walk. The driver of the Mustang didn't stop (hit and run), but the man and another woman wanted to call for an ambulance.

However, despite being in a daze I knew I didn't need one.

I thanked them for their help, picked myself up, and started walking again. By the time I got to the restaurant where my husband was waiting I looked normal. And as I sat down and recounted the experience, I knew I'd been fundamentally changed.

What is love?

During my near-death experience, I was exposed to an overwhelming recollection of (and gratitude for) all the love in my life. It was quickly followed by an experience of forgiveness that saw the cells of my body and my being release pain in the same way clouds release water droplets when they become too heavy.

And these truths became clear.

- **Love is all there is.** Our need for love is even more fundamental than our need for food or shelter.
- **Love restores reason.** We are all teachers and students, here to love and be loved. When we care and connect, we break patterns that don't have heart.
- **Love is connection** with ourselves and each other. The genesis of everything I do is to help

Our need for love is even more fundamental than our need for food or shelter.

you be more connected to yourself. And by being more connected to yourself, you can be more connected to others.

After my experience, I was driven to continue my quest to understand love better. I wanted to dissect it like an animal so I could get to the heart of it on a granular level.

One day I found myself walking a path I took almost every day. I asked nature:

"Where is love?"

"Like, where is it?"

"Show. Me. Love."

And suddenly, there it was in front of me—a heart-shaped opening created by two trees, their branches cradled over each other.

Wow.

Funnily enough, I never saw that "heart" opening again, despite repeatedly walking the same path. But here's what I took from that experience:

Love is everywhere.

It's like getting a new car. You never really noticed that model before, but now that you have one you see it everywhere. And when you open your eyes to love, you'll start seeing it everywhere because it is everywhere. You just need to be awake to it.

Those trees unlocked my awareness of love. And that in turn unlocked a sense that I was now *responding* to things rather than *reacting* to things.

This awareness completely changed my life without me having to change a thing.

With this awareness came a change in energy. A sense of flow, like a flower opening to the sun. There's no pushing or pulling. Just an innate potential coming into being.

I continued to study love. To seek the truth of it. And as I studied what the sages, mystics, and teachers have said over thousands of years, I found something they all agreed on:

Love is the ultimate truth.

Love stopped being a mystery to me. It stopped being something I was trying to reach for and hold on to. It stopped being something I was seeking and wanting to uncover. And it started being something that was just always *there*.

Moving toward what we love

When David became an avid mountain biker, I also became one because we do most things as a family.

At first I couldn't stop staring at the trees, hills, rocks, and bumps in the road.

"Your bike will go where your eyes go," David said. "If you stare at the obstacles, you'll crash right into them. If you want to move through the obstacles, look past them."

And he was right. Not only for mountain biking, but also for life.

His words reminded me of how I used to live my life. I was so focused on the obstacles that I'd always crash into them. During a period I call my "Dark Years", I was terrified to act because I was so fixated on avoiding mistakes.

Things got better only when I shifted my focus from what I *didn't* want to what I *did* want. Instead of focusing on:

- less sugar
- fewer dishes
- less confusion.

I focused on:

- more sunshine
- more time to read books
- more sleep.

The difference was subtle. But it was everything.

We generally run away from what we fear. But with training, we can rewire our brains so we run toward what we love instead. Until I started focusing on inviting the positive instead of avoiding the negative, I wasn't even living.

There's a story about twins who are told to enter a room where they'll receive a gift. When they arrive, there's a pile of horse dung on the floor.

The first twin throws a tantrum. "I thought we were getting a gift?!"

But the second one says, "Oh my, there must be a pony somewhere!"

Two people can see the same thing in entirely different ways. And while some of it may be genetic, reframing is a skill we can all cultivate. You can't always control what the world gives you, but you *can* control what you see and how you use what you're given.

Dr. Rick Hanson, psychologist and author of multiple books on positive neuroplasticity and the brain, explains it like this.

Your brain is like tofu—it takes on the flavor of anything you cook it with. When we allow our attention to default to fear, our brain gets used to fear. If we train ourselves to focus on gratitude, our brain starts to get used to gratitude.

On top of the tofu is a Dyson vacuum cleaner with a spotlight. Our attention is that spotlight, and you can point it wherever you want. But most of us don't realize we have the power to redirect the spotlight— so we go on pointing it at the negative.

We can choose to shift the spotlight and change our default.

I always thought I was wired for unhappiness. That something was wrong with me. But when I started learning about the actual science, I realized we're all wired with a negativity bias that evolved so we could protect ourselves.

When you realize it's human nature, and that you're not broken and don't need to be fixed, you can start feeling some compassion for yourself. Modern life is mostly safe, and we rarely need our negativity bias.

Whenever one of my young boys screamed, cried, or threw a tantrum, I'd get down on my knees so they could see we were on the same level. I'd then look them in the eye and ask three simple questions to see whether their basic needs were being met.

You don't need to be "fixed". That's an incorrect assumption that something is "wrong" with you.

"Are you hungry?"

"Are you tired?"

"Do you need a hug?"

We're so focused on fixing ourselves that we don't stop and ask ourselves, *are my basic needs being met?*

You don't need to be "fixed". That's an incorrect assumption that something is "wrong" with you.

You simply need to nurture love for yourself so you can recognize your wants and needs, and then meet them.

Accessing love

Over the years I've learned that to access love we need to unlock our awareness of our brain, body, and spirituality/presence to generate:

- gratitude
- forgiveness
- self-compassion.

Here are two exercises that will help you unlock that awareness.

Exercise 1 – Gratitude

Perform the following exercise each **morning**.

Think about three things or items in your day you can be grateful for.

Choose at least one thing that's:

- **routine** – an "everyday" thing (e.g., a safe place to sleep, food to eat, the sun supporting life on Earth).
- **specific** – a "unique to that day" thing (e.g., a friend who's doing you a favor, the weather allowing you to walk to work or get out for a run, the lunch break you'll be taking).

Make sure you highlight different things every day. (Don't reuse anything you've come up with before.)

You don't have to write them down (although I do encourage it). Simply bring each item to mind one at a time, and allow yourself to feel gratitude for each one.

How long you spend feeling that gratitude is up to you. It could be a few seconds. It could be longer.

Don't be afraid to experiment each day to find out what works best for you.

- Does it feel easier to keep a mental list rather than a journal?

- Does your exercise start before you reach for your phone?
- Are you reviewing your list and feeling gratitude while brushing your teeth?

Give yourself permission to experience this exercise differently and choose which works best for you. You can experiment and change anything about this exercise except:

- the types of things ("routine" and "unique to your day")
- the number of things (three).

And here's a similar exercise for you to perform each **evening**.

Think back over your day, and pick two "unique to that day" things you *could* have been grateful for but *weren't*.

Allow yourself to feel as much gratitude as possible for each of them.

Now recall an everyday thing you typically ignore and rarely feel grateful for.

And again, allow yourself to feel grateful for it.

Exercise 2 – Forgiveness

During my near-death experience, I was exposed to every form of love I'd given and received. Remembering and overwhelming my system with love led to what I can only describe as a "washing away" of pain—forgiving myself and others. It made me feel free, and allowed me to "dissolve" into a kind of formless mist before being jerked back into my body.

Over the years I've found ways to train or condition myself to either recall love or forgive myself and others.

One of these forgiveness practices comes from Dr. Jeffery A. Martin, a social scientist researching personal transformation and the highest levels of human well-being. He uses his research to make systems available that help people obtain profound psychological benefits rapidly, secularly, reliably, and safely.

Forgiveness is a gold standard exercise within positive psychology. It's a highly tested and reliable way to increase your well-being.

As with the gratitude exercise, this exercise has two parts. You do one when you wake up each morning, and the other just before you go to sleep each evening.

In the morning, choose one of three ways to reflect on and activate forgiveness:

1. Ask everyone you've ever harmed to forgive you, and forgive anyone who has ever harmed you. (This is the "general" form of the exercise.)
2. Get specific: Ask for forgiveness from specific people for a specific incident, and forgive specific people for specific incidents.
3. Do a mix of the first two.

The intent is simple:

- Forgive all those you have harmed.
- Forgive all those who have harmed you.

You can complete this exercise by making a simple mental, verbal, or written statement. If you want to go a little deeper, you can actively generate the *feeling* of forgiveness.

In the evening, look back on your day and look for specific examples of where forgiveness was needed. Forgive as many things as possible that happened in the day.

Important note: When referring to yourself, use "myself" in the statement (i.e., "I forgive myself.").

The truth of love is you can't truly love others until you love yourself.

Self-compassion

The longest journey of my life—the six inches from my head to my heart—started with years of research.

I wanted to know what the truth of love was. The Bible describes it differently to the movies, which in turn describe it differently to my friends and family.

Was I missing something?

When we first attempt to change, we're typically immersed in anger or blame. It's our spouse's fault or our parent's fault—anyone but ourselves. And for years I was like that too.

But at some point I put down the finger of blame and faced myself. I took responsibility for my problems, and for learning how to love myself first.

Before I started this journey, I thought prioritizing myself was selfish. Thankfully, I eventually found a simple answer:

The truth of love is you can't truly love others until you love yourself.

Becoming my own best friend was life changing. Before I prioritized self-love, I didn't realize how mean and judgmental I was being to myself. And that in turn limited my ability to give to others.

I used to be a lantern that would run out of oil. But when I started giving to myself, I became a candle that could give its light to others and still keep burning.

Self-compassion is the doorway to all positive transformation. In the Jewish tradition, compassion is the secret name for God.

What are you noticing in your heart right now? Keep asking yourself that question.

Are you noticing more compassion, or less? Can you shift your attention toward "more"?

Can you love yourself a bit more every moment?

Loving yourself is *simple*. But it's not *easy*. If it's something you struggle with, these exercises will help.

Exercise 1 – Cultivating compassion

This exercise is based on the Compassion Cultivation Training program at Stanford:

1. **Notice when you feel love, compassion, and kindness.** What thoughts are happening, and what emotions arise? What does it feel like in your body when they naturally occur? What does compassion feel like when you experience it? What are the physical and

physiological feelings of things like warmth, tenderness, or concern?

2. **Adopt a mindset of kindness and compassion.** Look for ways to interpret day-to-day experiences compassionately, such as being kind or accepting to people.

3. **Practice an act** of intentional kindness or compassion once a day.

Exercise 2 – Practicing self-compassion

Give yourself permission to notice and acknowledge your own suffering.

Don't avoid or try to suppress judgmental thoughts. Instead, recognize they're only thoughts or perspectives.

Practice being understanding, kind, caring, and compassionate toward your thoughts.

Practice recognizing you're not the only one experiencing this suffering. Use what arises in you to help you understand these same things are also arising in other people. This will help you develop compassion for yourself as you experience these feelings, and for those who also experience them.

Exercise 3 – Self-compassion letter (morning and evening exercise)

Write yourself a self-compassion letter in the morning.

Pick something you can show or give yourself kindness, love, caring, acceptance, or compassion about.

Writing the letter from the perspective of a trusted friend or family member may help. What would they tell you from the perspective of unlimited compassion?

Read the letter in the evening, and let the words sink in.

Exercise 4 – Act of intentional kindness

Practice an act of intentional kindness or compassion once a day by looking for a way to help, show appreciation for, or otherwise support someone.

Exercise 5 – Appreciation

Look for opportunities to really see, appreciate, and thank people who have played or are playing a key role in your life. When doing this, notice the sense of greater connection and care you feel.

Changing memories into love

When I had my near-death experience, I remember watching a ticker tape. As I did so, I re-experienced:

- every loving moment I'd ever had with everyone in my life
- every moment of joy and love I'd ever lived through.

I'll never be able to replicate what I experienced. But I found a simple exercise I'd like to introduce you to.

This exercise was created through the intuition of a brilliant physicist named Lester Levenson, who was sent home to die with a severe cardiac problem in 1952.

It's based on what we now know through modern psychology, cognitive science, and neuroscience. Unfortunately, none of this information was available then.

As Lester lay there waiting to die, he thought about his doctor sending him home and realized it was making him angry. After all, doctors are supposed to heal people, not send them home to die.

Of course, cardiac medicine was primitive in the early 1950s. And in realizing this, Lester understood that his doctor had probably done everything he could. He

Loving yourself is simple. But it's not easy.

wouldn't have enjoyed sending Lester home to die. Lester was certain his doctor got into medicine for the same reason every other doctor got into medicine: To save lives.

This realization forced a perspective change in Lester. And as part of that, he felt his anger change to love and compassion for the doctor. Moving from anger and resentment to love and compassion felt good, and so he began to test it with other memories from his life.

Lester's version involves systematically recalling memory after memory and transforming the emotion around each one into love. Some memories were quick. All he had to do was bring up the memory and ask himself, *Can I change this into love?* But others took more time.

To optimize this method, and get the most impact in the least amount of time, you won't be working with memories. Instead you'll be working with people, and all the memories, thoughts, and emotions you associate with them.

So the first thing to do here is make a list of people. Then, work through these three steps for each person on your list.

STEP ONE

Ask yourself: What feeling do I get when I think about the person?

Yes, it's that simple.

Recall the person's name, then simply pay attention to how you feel when you think about them.

STEP TWO

Ask yourself: Can I transform that feeling into love?

When you ask yourself the question, wait for a moment. (You can ask it more than once.)

By asking the question you're creating an intention. You want the feelings that show up to change into love.

If the feeling *does* turn into love, you've completed the exercise and it's time to move on to the next person.

But if the feeling *doesn't* turn into love, proceed to the final step.

STEP THREE

Actively generate love while you think about this person.

By doing this, you replace your current feeling for this person with a feeling of love. And in doing so it forces you to associate a new feeling with this person–love.

My own experience gave me a concentrated dose of this. The overwhelm of love produced a natural forgiveness that released me from that state of fear we default to as human beings.

Questions you may ask yourself during this exercise

Is this appropriate for people who don't deserve it?

Yes. Because remember, you're not loving this person for them and who they are. You're loving them for you. You're the only person holding the negative feelings you've associated with them. They don't feel it.

What kind of love should I feel?

Love shows up differently in our lives. Don't try to attain a specific version or experience of love. Any form of love will do.

Meditations on love

I've learned firsthand that the more love, trust, and care I give myself, the more I give to and receive from others.

The only way to learn this is by doing it through small daily actions that nurture and direct your attention.

The following meditations represent years of research and reading into what the truth of love actually is. Work through them as and when you need.

Meditation 1

The greatest kingdom one can reign over is the kingdom of the heart.

I promise to be honest with myself, listen to my intuition, and love myself.

I vow to cultivate a quality of sacred attention to the longing of the heart and the things I most deeply value.

I vow to listen to what the world is telling me with my whole being.

Meditation 2

Let us do by reason what pebbles and plants do by instinct and nature.

Let us move toward love.

What (small, tiny, itty bitty) action can I take to move forward?

What can I do to soften my heart to love?

Meditation 3

What small trigger in your life naturally opens you up to more love?

A certain kind of look from your partner?

A gesture that says, "I see you"?

A physical act like a hug?

Resolve to linger longer in those moments, and immerse yourself in that feeling of love.

Meditation 4

Love is the breath of life.

We have a personal obligation and responsibility to cultivate love, and to soften our hearts.

Ask yourself: why am I doing what I am doing today?

Take the time (invest it in yourself) to remember this practice in establishing a harmonious relationship with yourself or those around you.

We have a personal obligation and responsibility to cultivate love, and to soften our hearts.

Be curious, step back, and listen.

Notice.

Meditation 5

Allow the spirit of love to be in charge of your thoughts:

Moment by moment, you have a choice.

Moment by moment, you can decide.

You made a promise—a vow to grow your heart.

Congratulate and recognize your efforts.

If life has kept you from your promise, gently and without judgment put yourself back on the daily path of cultivating love.

Build a rhythm. Establish a new pattern. Train and prepare the mind to open your heart to your own knowing and understanding. Uncover your deeper inner wisdom and allow it to come forth.

Meditation 6

Moment by moment, you're allowing the spirit of love to be in charge of your thoughts. You're allowing it to open and soften your heart, and to illuminate the joy you can get from love.

Bring to mind your capacity to give and receive love instead of something you want, desire, or lack.

See and imagine the myriad facets of the diamond of love.

Meditation 7

Love never ends. It's not something that comes and goes like the wind.

Love is a choice you carry out in word and deed.

Love is a habit that takes you through the desert to the eternal oasis.

Expand your capacity to give and receive love.

Put your hand over your heart. (This releases the love hormone oxytocin.)

Breathe in and out through the center of your heart. (See or feel the breath moving through your heart.)

Touch, connect, give, and receive your own love.

Meditation 8

Be sensitive to the love you need and the love you give.

Stay in touch with yourself and your feelings.

Give of yourself without giving yourself away.

The origin of respect is to look again. "Look back at, regard, consider."

Take three deep breaths and, if you feel safe, look back at yourself in and through your mind's eye. Do you see your brilliance? Take a few minutes to consider your own sparkle.

Meditation 9

To see someone, look through your heart. You will uncover their truth and your own dynamic brilliance.

Intention for today: *May each step I take serve as a prayer, and each word I share as love.*

Meditation 10

Relax, take a deep breath, and move in the direction of your best self in harmony with the highest good for all concerned.

Ask yourself: *What is my growing love story today?*

Meditation 11

Love is learned best in wonder and joy, in peace, and in daily living.

What do you need from your own heart?

Time? Trust? Truth?

Tap into your inner wisdom.

Meditation 12

Courage = Heart.

An allegiance to self.

Deep compassion and love for self.

Fear – Love – Glory.

Allow what's been covering the truth of what you are to burn away.

Write it down.

Say it out loud.

Burn the paper and blow the ashes into the wind.

Meditation 13

To the extent that God has control of our hearts, you will have control of your life.

What is the lesson?

What forgiveness is needed?

Meditation 14

Who do you think you are?

Think about thinking.

You are an idea. You can change your thoughts of who you are and who you become.

What is the most loving thing you can do for yourself right now?

Meditation 15

Your true self has everything you need.

Remember your true nature.

Reconnect with God.

Recover your authentic happiness.

Discover your uniqueness.

Share your talents and gifts.

All relationships are teachers.

Your true self has everything you need.

Meditation 16

Finding joy in my relationships = finding joy in my life.

I am discovering the true wonder of me.

Not just the present me, but also the many possibilities of me.

Meditation 17

The greatest love affair of our life is with ourselves.

Go be yourself.

Be willing, without the need to be perfect.

Meditation 18

Ask yourself: is this going to make me feel better or worse?

Pause, then make a choice.

How do I make every day about loving?

Meditation 19

Love what is.

What is my soul urge?

Meditation 20

I am my first relationship.

I am whole.

There's nothing to get, only to allow.

I focus on my life's work, and allow others to do what's right for them.

Meditation 21

Shift from trying to *receive* love to wanting to *create* or *generate* love.

Be gentle with yourself.

Meditation 22

One loves because they will it.

One loves because it gives them joy.

One loves because they know their growth and discovery depends on it.

The only assurance we have lies within ourselves.

Eagerly accept all others can give, but be certain of and depend on nothing but the treasure of your inner self.

Do something that makes you laugh.

Meditation 23

Love is an act of faith, and whatever is of little faith is also of little love.

What makes your heart sing?

Meditation 24

The truth of love is that it's endless.

Love doesn't go away. But it might change form, like water.

Love is infinite. The relationship or the loving behavior can disappear, but never the love.

Love is unconditional. But while all love is true, it isn't always pure.

Access your heart intelligence.

Meditation 25

As a man thinketh in his heart, so is he.
~ James Allen, based on Proverbs 23:7

Love is the natural impulse of our heart.

Meditation 26

Witness.

Watch yourself.

Without judgment.

Tomorrow is another day.

With awareness comes compassion.

Meditation 27

Beliefs are not your fault. But they are 100% your responsibility.

Love grows more love.

Meditation 28

The inward journey is about finding our own fullness. Love has its own power.

No fear = freedom.

Meditation 29

The walls around your heart affect every area of your life.

Listen to love.

Meditation 30

I am creating room for love.

My relationship with myself is eternal.

I am my own best friend. I feel love soaking every cell of my body as I create a safe space for myself in love.

I draw loving people and loving experiences toward me.

I honor the truth of my heart.

Meditation 31

Do what you love, and love will find you.

Love is practice.

Meditation 32

Like freedom, love demands courage.

To change the love we receive, we must change our capacity to give love.

Do what opens your heart and serves the world.

To change the love we receive, we must change our capacity to give love.

Meditation 33

We can only be said to be alive in those moments when our hearts are conscious of our treasures.
~ Thornton Wilder

Love the life you live.

Live the life you love.

Meditation 34

Love can be easy.

Let it be easy.

We can become the love we want to find.

We can source it from within.

Start the day with intention. I wake up today with strength in my heart and clarity in my mind.

Reflection

Love yourself deeply, with forgiveness, and with compassion. Appreciate all your strengths, gently acknowledge your growth areas, and peacefully accept yourself for who you are.

Write down what you learned from this series of meditations.

Close your eyes, and take several deep breaths.

Open your eyes, and write whatever comes to you. It doesn't need to make sense. Just keep writing without reading what you write until your hand feels like it won't move any longer.

Delight in the wisdom that comes out. Copy any word or phrase that holds meaning for you.

FINAL REFLECTION: LOVE

You're not an individual living in your body, separate from the world and the people around you. Aligning your actions and intentions with the belief you are connected, shifts you from the trap of busyness to the depths of your true nature. You become deeply rooted in belonging; more authentically creative; connected to yourself, others and nature; doing work you're proud of; and creating a future you want to see.

SECTION 2

Being

"Understanding yourself is power. Loving yourself is freedom. Forgiving yourself is peace. Being yourself is bliss."

~ UNKNOWN

Being

I grew up poor. From middle school on, I picked cotton and worked other summer jobs to help pay for school clothes.

In contrast, when I was in my 30s I lived in a three-story house on a secluded hill with five bedrooms and a spectacular view. It had an office, a bar, a gym, a guest room, and so much space I can't remember what we did with it all. Nobody I knew had ever lived in such a luxurious house. I could barely fathom it.

One night, I was sitting in our hot tub overlooking the Franklin Mountains. It was a cool, beautiful desert night, and we lived far enough in the wilderness that we could see the stars and hear the wolves.

This was no ordinary hot tub either. It sat eight people comfortably, and my seat was custom-built for my body.

But I was shocked to find that I could have a house and a life that was literally beyond my wildest dreams, and still be miserable.

Sitting in the hot tub with a glass of wine in my hand and my butt snugly nestled into the custom seat, I looked out at the natural beauty while pondering this long period in my life (which I call "The Dark Night of my Soul"). The heavy sadness I felt at the time was growing stronger by the day (the wine may have had something to do with that), and I suddenly felt the need to tell someone I was struggling.

So I called my sister and my cousin.

I didn't know what to ask for, or even what to say. But I wanted to explore my feelings in a loving container. I wanted to admit to someone that I was struggling, despite my outward success.

When I told them what I was struggling with, they both laughed and made a joke.

"I wish I had your problems, Vivian."

That shut me up, both at that moment and for the couple of years after.

I continued living a life that looked perfect from the outside, but felt broken from the inside.

Was there something wrong with me? Did I just need to be more grateful and appreciate what I had? I kept torturing myself, asking why I couldn't be content.

Years later I discovered the answer.

There was *nothing* wrong with me.

I *didn't* need to shut up and appreciate what I had.

And the same goes for you.

Your friends and family can't feel what you feel. And they don't know what you know. When it comes to your inner world, no one on the outside can see what you see.

For me, it became clear I'd lost all sense of identity.

My husband had retired from the military. If I wasn't a military wife, who was I?

I'd resigned from a six-figure job. If I wasn't a successful consultant, who was I?

I'd completed my doctorate. If I wasn't a high-achieving student, who was I?

My children were leaving the house and heading out to the real world. If I wasn't an attentive mother, who was I?

I felt like I was losing myself.

Who was I beyond the roles I'd played my entire life?

My misery was perfectly fine. It was a natural expression of a life yet to be lived – a divine flame of discontent.

And how was I supposed to figure it out without sounding ungrateful to the people I loved–people who had "better" reasons to complain?

Now, there *was* something wrong with me as I sat in that hot tub, drinking wine, staring into beautiful mountains, and wondering why I was miserable.

But it wasn't the lack of gratitude I felt for everything I had.

Nor did it have anything to do with my husband, children, sister, cousin, or even my uncertainty.

No, the problem was that I thought I "should" be happy even though I wasn't.

My misery was perfectly fine. It was a natural expression of a life yet to be lived–a divine flame of discontent.

Spirituality is unique to everyone. But in my experience, we find ourselves drawn toward a kinder and more relational sense of the sacred–a spiritual life rooted in love and belonging.

In this space, we explore the wonder and mystery of life with a focus on the sacred in everyday experiences. We awaken through a spiritual path/practice in our daily life. These experiences transform into spiritual practices because they cultivate an expanded awareness that shifts your relationship to your thoughts, allowing them to flow without being carried away.

This section of the book is where we'll seek to awaken through presence and prayer using reflection exercises and meditations.

Start with your breath

A good way to help your mind and spirit be in the right frame for "being" is a short exercise I call *Reconnect*.

Reconnect

Here's how it works.

Close your eyes.

(Closing your eyes releases the pull of energy typically being drawn out of you.)

If you're sitting up, straighten your spine. If you're using your bed, the carpet, the ground, or the grass to support you, just let your spine stretch.

Using whichever hand feels most comfortable, place an open palm (skin to skin if possible) on your belly just above your navel. This will allow you to tune in to your root chakra.

Now place the thumb and forefinger of your other hand on your clavicle, just above your chest and just below your throat. This creates a closed circuit within your body.

Now, notice your breath.

Is it shorter?

Is it longer?

Did your mouth open or close?

Are you breathing through your nose?

Just take note of what your body is guiding you to do.

If there's tension in your shoulders, allow them to rest.

If there is tension in your jaw, allow it to move.

How does your neck like to support you? Is your chin up, toward the sky? Down, toward the earth? Again, just take note of what your body is guiding you to do.

Are your fingers spread wide across your skin, or are they closed?

Just take note.

And simmer there for six breaths.

Then slowly come back into some awareness. Move your top hand down to your belly, and your bottom hand up to your chest. Switch your arms, and pay attention to how that feels.

Are your elbows out and tense? Or have they stayed relaxed?

Notice how your posture shifts because of this movement.

Take three or four more breaths.

Then, whenever you feel ready, wiggle your fingers and slowly come back to full awareness.

Heart-focused breathing

Heart-focused breathing is about directing your attention to the heart area and breathing a little more deeply than normal.

Here's a summary of the simple steps.

Step 1: Focus on the area around your heart. Imagine your breath is flowing in and out of your heart or chest area as you breathe a little slower and deeper than usual.

Step 2: Activate and sustain a regenerative feeling such as love, appreciation, care, or compassion.

Step 3: Radiate that renewing feeling to yourself and others.

And here's a more detailed explanation.

I want you to bring your attention to the area around your heart.

Imagine your breath flowing in and out of your heart.

You might notice your breath slows down and becomes deeper than usual.

Allow that. You're going to be drawing your attention to your heart for at least two minutes.

Again, imagine your breath flowing in and out of your heart–heart-focused breaths, deepening, slowing.

Focus all your attention on your palm and heart area.

Take note of how you're feeling.

Imagine your breath flowing through your heart.

Lengthen your breath, and slow it down.

While focusing on your breath, imagine your heart, and your breath flowing through it.

Feel yourself shifting into a more coherent state.

Coherence allows love, appreciation, and courage. It's the alignment of your heart, your mind, and your emotions.

And it can be measured.

This calm, comfortable, chilled feeling you feel right now is where you grow.

This is a space where we can learn. If we're feeling anxious, worried, irritated, frustrated, tired, or angry, that's the off switch. Nothing generative happens there. Your mind and all your faculties shut down to just keep you safe. This is the state where you can grow.

Take a couple more deep breaths while imagining your breath flowing through your heart, and then come back.

Have a nice, big yawn.

Okay.

And remember: This calm, comfortable, chilled feeling you feel right now is where you grow.

Releasing breath

Every breath we let go is "releasing" in nature. With that in mind, I want you to bring some awareness to your own inhaling and exhaling.

Lengthen your breaths with intention.

Take note of the rhythm of your breathing.

Imagine the breath moving through your heart.

Inhale.

Exhale.

Inhale.

Exhale.

Gently bring to your awareness a feeling of appreciation, care, and compassion. It can be a reflection on something you're grateful for, or someone you feel close to.

Hold whatever brings you a feeling of compassion, care, or appreciation in your heart.

Take two more breaths in that place, then come back.

Beautiful.

Basic meditation exercise

Start by getting comfortable.

Feel the sensation in and around your nose as your breath flows in and out of it.

Focus on your nose, and note the sensation you feel.

That's it. That's the entire exercise.

Set a timer and give it a try.

Expect your mind to wander. Return your attention to the exercise and continue.

When most people start a meditation practice, their mind naturally starts looking for progress. *Am I doing it right? Maybe I'm doing it wrong. What if I'm not doing it right? Should my eyes be closed?*

You should try to keep those types of things out of your mind as much as possible. Don't compare or second-guess yourself. Just do it.

The simple practice is designed to train your brain and build your introspection skills.

Often your mind will be telling you, *It can't be this easy! There must be something I'm doing wrong.* Ignore your mind if it tries to compare, doubt, and worry about how well it's going and whether you're doing it correctly.

Follow the basic instructions, resist your mind's attempts to distract you, and just keep going. There's no way you can get it "wrong".

The practice really is as simple as it seems. Feel the sensation in and around your nose as your breath flows in and out of it.

As you meditate, try to "watch" your thoughts come and go.

Watch the worry or concern come and go. You need to maintain a degree of self-control so you can distance yourself from your thoughts and emotions by just watching them.

That may not seem easy, or even possible, when you first start out. That's fine.

What you don't want is to let your thoughts and emotions stop you. And you don't want to feed them by engaging with what your mind is trying to convince you of, either.

Your best option is to simply ignore what your mind is trying to tell you.

Watch the mental processes unfold and get some distance from them by just "watching" your thoughts as they occur.

However, there is one exception. If you experience a significant negative psychological event, such as an intense negative emotional response or trauma, you should talk to a professional.

The meditation instructions are to pay attention to the sensation in and around your nose as your breath flows in and out of it.

If something distracts you, just watch that thought, emotion or sensation arise. Don't judge yourself for having that thought. Your brain is just doing what it's supposed to. Just observe it, and then bring yourself back to focusing on your breath.

It's all part of the process and your wiring. It's not anything to judge or be frustrated by.

Posture

You should do whatever feels most comfortable.

Whether you lay down, sit in a comfy chair, or adopt an Eastern type of meditation posture, is of no importance.

You simply need to be comfortable.

Timing

When should you meditate? I recommend you experiment with meditating at different times of the day. Try mornings, afternoons, and evenings. As you experiment with different times, you'll find one that works better than the others.

Location

You should also experiment with different locations to see which one works best for you.

Use trial and error to figure it out.

The main point is to practice. Focus on the exercise, and ignore things like:

- your ideas about it
- your thoughts about the results
- the lack of results/your expectations
- comparisons with other things you've done.

Don't try to figure anything out. Just do the practice.

Any time you hear a "should", think of it as an invitation to explore.

Release yourself from the "shoulds"

When I think back to the "Dark Night of my Soul", I now see there was nothing "wrong" with me or that needed to be different. The divine discontent was simply a signal of my own growth potential.

The solution was simple: I needed to stop "shoulding" myself.

Whenever you're in a period of uncertainty, your mind starts telling you what you *should* do. But the voice of "should" is never your voice. It's the voice of your parents. Of culture. Of society.

Think of it as a game. Any time you hear a "should", think of it as an invitation to explore.

Who's doing the "shoulding"?

Is this "should" aligned with something you genuinely want? Or is it someone else's idea?

If the "should" isn't completely aligned with what you want, release yourself from it.

"Shoulds" come from without.

"Wants" come from within.

In my experience, "shoulds" tend to shout loud when what you want is unconventional. The mainstream voice (the "should") is worried you might fail, stand out, or be judged as different.

Your "should" is trying to protect you.

But you don't need its protection. **Living your truth isn't as dangerous as your mind thinks it is.** This type of failure won't kill you.

On the other hand, living a life of "shoulds" is a slow spiritual death.

If you follow your "shoulds", nothing you achieve will ever feel meaningful because you'll be achieving somebody else's goals instead of your own.

Don't worry about what you *should* do. Just identify what you *want* to do, and do it.

For the first 40 years of my life, all I did was follow my "shoulds". I wound up with everything society told me I *should* want, and yet I was miserable.

That night in the hot tub, all I could think was that I *should* be happy. But like my wine that carried undertones of vanilla, my "shoulds" came with undertones of shame, anger, and Catholic guilt. I'd checked all the boxes to be happy, and yet I still wasn't.

Years later, I figured out how to ask better questions.

Who's telling me I should be happy?

What do I want instead?

In all those years of focusing on other people's dreams, I never thought about what I wanted for myself.

I remember sitting outside with David on a warm, summer evening. We'd been bickering a lot, but that night we were having a nice conversation. Still, something felt off. And I couldn't keep it to myself.

"I don't think I can be happy with you," I said. "I don't think I can grow into the person I'm supposed to be with you around."

Luckily for me, David stayed calm and listened *beyond* my words.

"If you'll truly be happier without me, then that's what I want too," he said. "All I want is for you to be happy."

His calmness snapped me back into reality. I certainly wasn't sure leaving my husband would make me happier. I needed to slow down before I really screwed something up.

I came to realize I'd been pointing fingers at everyone around me, instead of turning my attention inward. That was the peak of the "Dark Night of my Soul"–the years where I lived with a constant sense of dread, feeling as if I was about to do something I'd regret for the rest of my life and having just enough strength to stop myself from going through with it.

But no solutions came, and nothing seemed to improve. I just sat there, praying that the storm would pass.

Eventually, I enrolled in a ten-day silent meditation retreat to try and figure things out. No technology, writing, or even speaking. Just meditating for ten hours a day.

Well, that's not strictly true. We had a few minutes of free time each day. And I spent that time walking the property, sitting on my favorite bench, and praying. I needed to figure this thing out. *What's the right thing to do?* I didn't want to do something I'd regret.

I constantly asked myself questions. But no answers came.

On the final day, I decided to just listen. I guess the retreat did what it was supposed to because I finally let myself be silent. I finally let myself just "be".

Walking away from that bench for the last time, I looked back for some reason and saw something I'd never noticed. The "tree" I'd sat under for ten days was actually two different trees that had grown together. And they both seemed to be very healthy and happy.

I think those trees saved my marriage.

Up to that point, I'd never seen a real-life example of two things growing individually yet remaining healthily intertwined. Finally, something spoke to my heart and showed me I could have personal fulfillment *and* a successful marriage.

Since we weren't allowed to use phones or write at the retreat, I took a picture of the tree with my mind instead. When I returned home I told David about it, and he loved it.

I told him that before seeing the tree I was convinced we had to break apart to grow. But once I'd seen it I knew we could grow separately, together.

I'd been too frightened to act until I had an answer because I didn't want to mess anything up. But once I stopped asking for an answer and just listened to whatever arose, I got one.

My "Dark Years" were like a real-life storm—one where you need to wait for the lightning and thunder to pass before you go anywhere.

I had no idea what I was doing. But through God's grace, divine intervention, or whatever it was, I didn't act. I cried and agonized as the storm raged around me, but fortunately I didn't mess anything up.

If you're going through your own "Dark Night of the Soul", picture the storm. Don't blow up your life. Just

Until we make space for the voice of the divine to speak, we'll never know where to go or what to do.

wait until it passes. If you don't have a hint or thread of what's right for you, don't do anything.

Make space to listen.

When the storm was raging, and the tears were flowing, I knew I needed a place to feel safe and wait out the storm. So I created a prayer room in my house, where I could sit, pray, and cry in silence.

It was my sanctuary.

When I couldn't cope with life, or didn't know what to do, I ran to the prayer room. There I could be alone and wait, without any expectations from anyone. And it felt like my prayers held me as I waited for answers.

We live in an impatient society. Figuring out your life's direction takes time. When we rush our decisions, we make mistakes. When we listen for answers, they come … eventually. But we can't control divine timing.

If your life is in danger, you need to take immediate action. But if you're having a "Dark Night of the Soul", there's no danger in waiting.

The answer will come eventually. Don't force it.

Until we make space for the voice of the divine to speak, we'll never know where to go or what to do. But once we start to hear it, we can confidently take steps while it guides us.

Spiritual growth isn't a race. And you can't run toward your answers before you learn to listen for them where you are right now.

A transformative change of heart

In this section I'll be sharing thoughts and meditations you can contemplate at your own pace over the course of one or more days. These thoughts, questions, and actions seek to:

- evoke wonder and wisdom
- invite authentic self-expression
- allow for a wider, deeper, and more open awareness.

Let's begin.

1.

We're all guided by candlelight.

We're all learning to walk in the shadows a few steps at a time, getting comfortable with the fact there's little certainty in life.

You're forging your own personal path forward.

Allow lots of time for integration.

Change is tough. But it's worth the effort.

2.

Instead of always looking for the "right answer", pay closer attention to the *questions* you're asking.

Name and take note of what you're asking. And then give yourself enough time to let the answers show up for you.

You can wade out into the ocean from the shore. Or you can wait for the wave to come in and carry you out.

3.

Dante opens Inferno with these words:

> *I found myself within a forest dark,*
> *For the straightforward pathway had been lost.*

Even if you can't see anyone else on the pathway, you share it with others.

This is our journey.

It's the journey of our life, between the known and the unknown.

It's the "in between".

4.

I have a metaphor for you. Compare the continuous straight line that's always moving forward to the spiral or curved line that turns toward itself.

The challenge is to find a continuous straight line that's always moving forward in nature. My hunch is you can't find one. That's not how Mother Nature works.

Our critical left brain continuously drives us forward, seeking direct routes and unending progress. It always wants to go further, faster, and in the same direction.

It's slightly different to integrate some of your right brain and think in a more circular fashion because there are no straight lines in nature, instead, they always and ultimately return to their origins.

So if as humans we think a circle is more natural than a straight line, we can see we'll come back to that from which we came.

Sometimes I get frustrated when I forget something I've learned. But when I look at the experience, I can see I've moved a bit deeper and a bit closer to my center, like the rings of the tree.

Everything in nature lives, grows, develops, and expands from within. And we're designed to do the same.

Thanks to recent scientific breakthroughs, we've moved from Newtonian (linear and direct) physics to looking at the world through more of a quantum view (where we're in flow and profoundly connected).

And maybe we can shift how we see ourselves as well. Instead of being a body that simply ages, maybe we can be more like Heraclitus's River–always flowing but always the same, always changing but always itself.

5.

Repetition doesn't always mean redundancy.

You always gain new insight when you revisit something, whether it's a movie, a book, or even a memory. Whenever I re-read a book I seem to hear, pull out or highlight new words. I learn something new every time.

6.

Allow yourself to rest on the journey.

Pause, slow down.

Test this against your own experience.

Pause.

Let it sink in, then ask yourself, *What am I curious about? What sounds true to me?*

If none of the ideas or invitations spur your natural curiosity, let them all go.

Change is a process that requires repetition over time.

Take note of what's already stirring your heart, and reflect on that.

I'm here to help you remember what you already know, not teach you something new.

You are your own best teacher.

Change is a process that requires repetition over time.

7.

Consider this perspective on cultivating your inner life by Guy Finley.

> "There is a significant difference between 'self-improvement' and real spiritual transformation. To understand this difference, consider the following: A newly opened rose is not an improved bud; this naturally fragrant expression of beauty and grace blossoms on its own when sunlight stirs its bud into awakening.
>
> Learn to stand in the light of self-awareness. Welcome its soul-stirring touch regardless of what it reveals within you. Yes, there are thorns; it hurts when we see that we are nothing like what we have taken ourselves to be. But no dream comes to an end without an awakening. And just as the rose takes the place of the bud, so will your newly opened heart take the place of fear and pain; a whole new you will show itself as having always been there, just waiting to flower."

Slow down enough to catch up with yourself.

8.

Release your need for certainty.

A few years ago, I started a nightly ritual of watching the moon shed its shadow. My intention was to release my own need for certainty—my own need for reaching for knowing.

This ritual has evoked wonder and wisdom, and allowed a wider, deeper, and more open awareness for insights to emerge.

When you release yourself from needing certainty, you open yourself up to remarkable insights.

9.

What are you intentionally willing to let go of?

Turn inward. Know yourself. Rest, don't rush. Insights will emerge if you're willing.

10.

Cultivate a life of contemplative prayer—a direct relationship with the divine. Whether you found yourself here or it's something you chose, allow a wider, deeper, and more open awareness. Insights will emerge.

The Texas Two-Step

Growing up in Texas, I loved watching people dance, whether it was the Two-Step or the Cumbia.

It fascinated me how they could move forward and all around the dance floor by taking one step forward and two steps back. And it helped me understand that when I take two steps back it's not failure. It's just part of the dance.

That backward step is a necessary pause before moving forward again.

When I told my sister and cousin I was struggling, I took a step forward, fueled by a surge of courage. When they laughed I took a step back, retreating into a pool of guilt and confusion.

Then the "Dark Night of my Soul" came. My second step back.

If I knew then what I know now, I would have recognized it as a pause. The pause before moving around the dance floor with joy, knowing the difference between wanting to go forward in a straight line and wanting to deepen my experience of living with greater meaning.

My feelings of guilt and shame weren't needed. And neither are yours.

But you won't feel liberated from the pull of obligations and other people's expectations until you start seeing life as a dance with steps both toward and away from your desires. There's a natural flow of moving back and forth.

The Texas Two-Step is a law of nature. There's no such thing as constant, linear progress.

Start recognizing the rhythm and flow of your heart. Don't move forward until you're ready. Don't avoid the pause.

You wouldn't go for a walk in thunder, lightning, and heavy rain. You'd wait for the storm to subside and the weather to pass. Life's no different. The pauses are part of our experience.

In *The Upside of Stress*, Kelly McGonigal explains that "stress may be a natural byproduct of pursuing difficult but important goals." That doesn't mean every stressful moment is rich and meaningful. But it *does* mean that even if the stress doesn't feel meaningful, it can be the trigger you need to start seeking and creating meaning.

Stress challenges us to find meaning in our lives. Fortunately, my stress drove me deeper into self-inquiry.

Stress can awaken your soul if you're willing to dig within. Don't refuse the call.

Your soul knows where to go

When we're struggling with our sense of "being", we tend to get caught up in our heads. And in doing so, we forget something crucial: When you let your soul guide the way, you can be confident the path you're on is aligned with your true values and desires.

Here are some exercises to help your soul light the way forward.

Exercise: Imagine your ideal

Imagine your way to a brighter future, or to becoming a better you. Together we'll build our creative muscles over the course of 14 exercises. These exercises will help you transform dust into glitter just by turning it slightly in the light.

1.

Thanks for being brave. Venturing out into the unknown can be scary.

I'd like to start by reminding you there are no rules in this space. Setting your sights on a faraway star is the reason we're here together right now.

Let your dream be big and wild. It will beckon you,

Following our heart and realizing our ideal is what fulfills us and gives us a sense of meaning.

and compel you forward. For us humans, following our heart and realizing our ideal is what fulfills us and gives us a sense of meaning.

Try to be playful and fun. Ignore the "how" and the logical details for now. This is a time for feeling, not thinking.

Let's start with three easy steps.

1. Choose a future you want.
2. Decide what parts of the past get to come along for the ride.
3. Use the present to make the best possible progress.

For shits and giggles, let's also be kind to ourselves. There's no right or wrong in this dream–this future tomorrow you're bringing to life. Let the energy of your wanting move you forward.

2.

What do you want?

Make a list.

Write without hesitation for five minutes, and fill at least one page with your desires. Review your list. Circle one desire that pulls at your heartstrings.

This is your guiding star in the dark sky. Allow it to beckon you, and compel you forward.

3.

Are doubts starting to creep in? If so, congratulations. You're officially normal.

It's our nature as human beings to move away from fear. We want to feel safe. The brave thing to do is a very different movement. It's a shift to seek out joy, love, and inner peace instead of running from what scares you or might be holding you back from what you know is truly meant for you.

Observe your hesitation.

What stands between you and your dream?

Is it real? Is it an immediate and present danger?

If it's not, then it's simply an illusion.

You can look at an illusion, and see through it like a stained-glass window. It colors your world and your experience.

What do you want to see?

Give yourself permission to hope, and to make your way toward your dreams coming true. Don't be afraid.

4.

Do you remember the story of King Midas?

He was granted one wish, and he wished for everything he touched to turn to gold.

At first, he was delighted, and was soon surrounded by luxurious precious metals and shiny brightness.

But it also meant anything he tried to eat or drink also turned to gold. And he soon realized he was destined to die of hunger and thirst.

The moral of the story is that the things we think will bring happiness and fulfillment won't always make us feel happy or fulfilled.

What we truly yearn for are verbs, not nouns. We're being beckoned by feelings.

Take a look at your list.

Imagine you've already achieved everything on that list.

Try to imagine how you'd feel if all the dreams you wrote down have already come true.

Beside each item on your list, write down one or two feelings that best describe the state you'll be in when you achieve it.

5.

When I was young, someone asked me if I was going to college. I'd always had a thing for travel and adventure, so I said, "Yes."

As the years went by, I imagined myself going on a road trip to San Antonio, Texas. I'm pretty sure I saw a place on the map called College Station, and figured that's where I'd be going.

(I later learned it wasn't quite what the person was asking, but the idea stuck with me. At the time I didn't know their idea of "going to college" was getting a four-year degree. I thought it was a place on the map everyone seemed interested in, and thought I should go there too.)

It stuck.

"College" became this guiding star that made everything in my life easy. Would the decision I was about to make lead me toward college or away from it? Would it support my success in college or not?

While going to college may not sound like a big deal, my parents never finished high school and were only first-generation literate in English. For me, even saying it was a bit of a stretch.

I'm encouraging you to stretch as well.

I firmly believe that God (or whatever name you call the divine) answers our prayers in one of three ways:

1. "Yes."
2. "Not yet."
3. "No, because I have something better in store for you."

So ask for exactly what you want, even if you have no idea how it will happen.

Believe, and reach for the shining star you've chosen to guide you forward.

6.

Is your dream starting to crystallize?

Seeing your dream become real, and knowing what it looks like, helps you get out of your own way.

If you know how something will feel before it happens, it not only helps you treasure it now but also guides you toward making it a reality.

Nothing's worth doing, or is big enough to be interesting, if it doesn't fail initially.

7.

Nothing's worth doing, or is big enough to be interesting, if it doesn't fail initially. Just keep working at it. This is where you become your own hero.

Even though I help people dream, that's only the first step in this process. Now it's time to make your dream a reality.

As you prepare your psyche to move forward, think about how you can move forward without fear.

Break down your dream into itsy bitsy teenie weenie yellow polka dot … wait, that's a song lyric.

Think of one small step you can accomplish in 15 minutes without any additional resources or skills.

But before we start …

Wait! You didn't start moving toward your dream without me, did you?

To make your ideal true, or your wildest dreams a reality, you need to be willing to feel the full range of feelings on your way there–the self-doubt, the darkness, and even the fear.

Are you willing to feel that?

And it's okay if it feels a little uncomfortable. That just means it matters to you in some way.

8.

Can I make a suggestion? It's a simple one. But keep in mind that simple things aren't always easy.

When you practice your thing, you'll be moving toward what makes you uncomfortable. So I suggest you keep practicing until it's no longer uncomfortable.

9.

Never in my wildest dreams did I think I'd ever be living the life I have right now. Anyone with a logical mind would think it was impossible.

Which goes to show that what you want is possible.

If you dream it, you can make it come true. And your reality can and will be even better than what you imagined.

Your beloved activity is both scary and exciting.

10.

Until we wake up, we're asleep to what's true for us.

Awaken yourself to what consciousness pioneer Barbara Marx Hubbard calls "the essential self", our truest state of being.

Your essential self doesn't care about things that seem to matter on the surface, such as matching socks or combed hair. Often the noise those things create muffles the signals your essential self is sending you.

What's one thing you would do if you could guarantee you wouldn't be judged by anybody (or at least the important people in your life)?

Dig in a little deeper, without any rules or judgment.

11.

Shift your attention away from what you're trying to avoid to what you want to make a reality.

Now re-read that sentence.

That attention shift is what changed my life a few years ago. I started moving toward love instead of away from fear.

As M. Scott Peck said in *The Road Less Traveled*, "Courage is not the absence of fear; it is the making of action in spite of fear."

Feel your soul's desire now.

12.

Yes, the struggle is real.

But so is the reward.

Dreaming big isn't foolish or silly, nor is it a waste of time. And *not* dreaming doesn't stop you from falling or being hurt.

It's your soul drawing you in and compelling you forward.

13.

If you follow your desires deeply enough, you'll find they ultimately stem from one of the soul's four true desires:

1. become who you're meant to be, and fulfill your unique purpose
2. have the material means to fulfill your purpose (money, health, and energy)
3. participate fully in life and experience its many forms of joy
4. become "soul-realized", and experience ultimate freedom from all forms of fear.

When your desires and goals are tied directly to one of these, your efforts will be fueled by true, clean and pure "soul fuel" rather than fast-burning, pollution-creating "personality desire fuel".

14.

In any given moment, we have a little voice in our head telling us what we need to do next, whether it's putting in a load of laundry, writing an email, or changing the world. There's always *something* that needs to be done. And you pretty much always know what that something is.

If you listen to that voice, you'll be in pretty good shape.

So what needs to be done right now? Not in ten years, or even ten minutes, but right at this moment.

Whatever it is, do it.

And then repeat these steps for the next thing. And the next. And so on.

"What" questions help you create a different possibility.

Exercise: Ask better questions

Asking questions is an important principle, and a way for you to build your perspective. Choose the path of inquiry to explore your inner life and see your outer world differently. This will awaken your wonder, and lead you to the *big* questions that will help you decide where to go next.

Questions are a great way to engage with yourself, and to start having conversations with yourself.

What kind of questions? "What" questions.

I prefer these to "Why" questions, which tend to trap us in the rearview mirror and create "analysis paralysis".

"What" questions, on the other hand, are more likely to move you forward. They help you understand who you are, what you want, and the kind of life you want to lead.

"What" questions help you create a different possibility.

Here are some "What" questions that can awaken you to a greater sense of self and being.

- What do you want for yourself? (Try not to fall in the trap of answering this question with what your parents, your beloved, or society in general wants for you, or expect you to wish for yourself. What do you want?)

- What would giving yourself permission to want more than you already have mean to you?
- What's getting in your way?

These questions are the first steps toward:

- cracking through the walls of what you already know and believe
- identifying what you need to unlearn.

But "unlearning" doesn't mean "forgetting", it simply means choosing a different mental model.

For example, I used to think a "good" wife enjoyed being in the kitchen. This was so far from my own personal truth that just thinking about it gave me physical pain. It was a lie I didn't even realize I was telling myself.

Once you're on the path to "unlearning" you can answer these questions:

- What do you want to let go of?
- What would be better?
- What's your "if-then" plan? (e.g. "If _____ then I will _____ [action to overcome the habit/thought pattern].)

Dare yourself to think not only bigger, but also differently.

Exercise: Imagine your possibilities

Imagining your possibilities is what I call "a workshop for your soul".

We can create the change we want. But before we can create that change, we need to decide what that change will be.

You've decided to go on a tiny little quest. And you've been cultivating the inner landscape. Now it's time to move out of our exterior world into stillness and silence, and allow our inner knowing to emerge.

This is where you'll discover your greatest potential. It's where you access your highest future possibility, and the truest expression of your unique and holy soul.

Continue bringing yourself to a calm, relaxed state.

You're going to step into a vision you're creating for your own life.

And you're going to dream your way there.

This is not the time for logic. Logic only creates barriers in this space.

This is your daydream time.

Your mind has limits for good reason: It's trying to protect you. It doesn't want you to be hurt or disappointed.

But in this space that's okay.

Ask your mind to take a break. Tell it (and yourself) that everything's okay. You're just going to dream for a bit.

Give it permission to let you go so you can set your own compass and orientate yourself as a wayfarer toward your highest value and your highest virtue.

Lengthen your exhales, and start centering yourself.

Reach beyond those first-level desires. You want your pure potential to bubble up from your soul.

The most important thing I discovered about being in this space is I can envision so much. I know there's even more beyond the horizon my mind hasn't even begun to dream about.

And I can do it without losing my gratitude for where I am now, or my engagement with where I am now.

When I started dreaming, my biggest obstacle was feeling selfish and ungrateful for what I already had, who I already was, and how I already served.

Moving toward what set my soul on fire was a beautiful experience. I could see that it served everyone from a place of peace, a place of calm, and a place of potential that wasn't selfish.

Exercise: MINE goals trump SMART goals

Let's explore the shift that's happening for you from a position of potential and possibility.

When you look at things from this position, you might use the word "dreaming".

> *What am I dreaming about making happen?*
>
> *What am I dreaming about shifting/creating in my life?*

What I'm about to share is an important principle in *Love Being Human*. And I need to share it with you so that you can explore it and see whether it works for you.

Before you set a goal or decide what you want, you need to ask yourself, *What do I value most in my life?*

And then explore those values around an aspiration–the guiding star you're moving toward as you move through your experience.

I often distinguish aspiration from achievement or ambition. It's as if you're in a boat, and you've identified an island you're moving to. Your focus is on getting to that island, right? Everything is about getting to the island. The island is the internal compass that tells you how to steer the ship. It's what keeps you moving in the right direction.

Let joy be your guiding star, not fear.

In life, values act in the same way. They recognize you and the experience you're having, guided by your internal compass as you move through the world. Focusing on imagination is about identifying the potential and the possibilities in front of you.

When we learn about setting goals here in the Western world, we're often told they need to be SMART:

- Specific
- Measurable
- Achievable
- Relevant
- Time-bound.

But while I can see the merits of setting SMART goals, that method has never resonated with me. And if it doesn't resonate with you either, then you might want to try setting them using the MINE acronym instead:

- Movement
- Innovation
- Nature
- Energy.

Here's what they all mean.

Movement: Move toward what you enjoy

What will this goal move you toward?

Will it move you toward joy? Toward love? Toward feeling more alive?

Or are you avoiding something, and moving away from things you fear?

Let joy be your guiding star, not fear.

This movement also signifies a commitment to a continuous journey rather than a destination.

Innovation: Make sure it's new, original, and specific to you

Innovation means your goal must be creative and original. How can you combine your DNA with the spices of your soul, personality, values, and purpose to find a goal that's unique to you?

Or how can you achieve an "ordinary" goal in a unique way?

Nobody in this world can create or become like you.

Does your motivation come from an internal aspiration? Or is it coming from what society says you should do?

Nature: Know that being scared is natural, but you can move through the fear

Fear is your brain telling you that you're doing something new and don't know how it will unfold. There's no danger, just uncertainty.

Recognize that you're going somewhere you've never been before. You can think of it as danger or an adventure. While we're naturally inclined to look for safety, we're also naturally inclined to explore.

Embrace the brave part of your nature.

Embrace the uncertainty. Embrace not knowing how it will go. Embrace feeling wobbly and then ground in your values. Rest when you need. Nurture yourself. Follow your guiding star of joy.

Remember: You're a human being, not a human doing. You're not a noun. You're a verb–continuously becoming, unfolding, and changing.

Energy: Block time according to your energy

SMART goals are time-based. But MINE goals are energy-based.

Racing against the clock doesn't add value to your life. It just adds unnecessary stress.

Instead of racing the clock, connect to your own energy flow. What's your rhythm? How and when do you work best?

The power of igniting your imagination

At the end of 2018, I looked back at the year and how wonderful it was. And then I started imagining what I wanted to move toward in 2019.

At this point my husband had been retired from the military for more than seven years. And I'd spent that time struggling with losing both my military community and my identity as a military spouse.

I had friends all over the world. Unfortunately, not many of them were geographically close.

So as I looked at 2019, I set myself a goal to cultivate my life in the real world, including my "in real life" relationships.

My coach at the time asked what I wanted this "in real life" thing to look like.

I answered with some realistic things I was confident I could create.

But then they asked, "What's your out-of-this-world wish?"

Interestingly, I already knew the answer. It's something I'd wanted for a long time, but had never given myself permission to move toward.

I wanted to become the host of CreativeMornings Fort Worth.

CreativeMornings is the world's largest face-to-face creative community. And back then Fort Worth didn't even have a chapter, let alone a host.

To produce CreativeMornings you need an entire team, as well as significant support from your local community and partners. But I didn't really know anyone in Fort Worth, and so my idea seemed like a complete moonshot.

But my idea never died because it aligned perfectly with my value of rising and shining in every imaginable way–waking people up, giving them inspiration, and creating a place where people could find the courage to do whatever they wanted.

It was also a way for me to make more "in real life" friends in Fort Worth who shared my worldview. People drawn toward creativity, possibility, bravery, courage, and just being themselves.

Allowing yourself to dream and ignite your imagination is so important.

In 2019 I gave myself permission to ignite my imagination, and pursue this seemingly impossible dream.

Within a few weeks of my decision, the Dallas chapter of CreativeMornings sent out an email asking whether anyone would be interested in bringing a chapter to Fort Worth.

The first initial meeting was on 31 January 2019. And before the meeting was over I was nominated for and accepted as the first host of CreativeMornings Fort Worth.

There was nothing realistic about my goal of becoming the host of CreativeMornings Fort Worth. But it became possible because I:

- allowed myself to hope
- allowed myself to believe it was possible
- gave myself permission to have that experience.

Allowing yourself to dream and ignite your imagination is so important.

It doesn't have to be profitable. It doesn't even have to be logical. But you need to align your goals with what matters to you, and what you want to bring into being.

You need to incorporate imagination, possibility, and potential into what you want to bring to the world.

If I'd stopped short, not thought about what would be perfect for me, and not brought this intention into form, I wouldn't be where I am now.

After that initial meeting, a group of us worked together to put the application video together. (It was a lot of work.)

We submitted the application.

I interviewed with headquarters.

In July, we were made an official chapter. And on 25 October we set the first meeting for CreativeMornings Fort Worth.

One of the most critical things to being happy is having face-to-face social interactions.

CreativeMornings has given me what I wanted. But it has also given something to our city. It has helped creatives rise, and created a space where we can have face-to-face conversations and share inspiration.

I'm sharing this story because I don't want you setting any goals without imagination. I want your goals to align with your values. I want you to draw them from your values so they become a unique fingerprint of who you are and what you want to bring into the world.

I'm inviting you to ignite your own imagination. I want you to feel confident you can create what you believe, and then act courageously to get it done.

FINAL REFLECTION: BEING

Being is the peaceful sea of a cultivated, meditative mind. It's our most valuable formless skill. Everything is unity. Our deepest desires draw us into peace, presence, and oneness. Truth is the gap between thoughts, feelings, and experiences.

SECTION 3

Human

> "There is some kind of a sweet innocence in being human—in not having to be just happy or just sad—in the nature of being able to be both broken and whole, at the same time."
>
> ~ C. JoyBell C.

Human

When I started my doctoral studies, I hoped graduation would be the final piece of my happiness puzzle.

I felt I'd ticked the boxes of "successful enough" and "loving enough". I'd experienced career success. My family was still together. My kids were healthy and doing well.

All I needed to complete the set was to be "smart enough". And that would happen the moment they handed me that final diploma.

Toward the end of the program, we were asked to prepare 50 words to address the audience at the graduation ceremony. I'd always felt a sense of relief at my previous ceremonies, immediately followed by impending doom. *Ugh. Time to start again for that next piece of paper.*

But this time there was no "next piece of paper". What do you do after getting a doctorate?

There's nothing you *can* do.

I started to panic.

Would I really feel "smart enough" just because I had my "final" degree? Would I magically know everything, and no longer need to learn? The last degree I'd completed obviously wasn't enough. Why would this one be any different?

A previous version of me would have spiraled at this point. Fortunately, at this point in my life I'd already done a lot of the work that you're doing now, and so I managed to talk myself out of spiraling.

I reminded myself that my entire education journey had been wonderful. And this final diploma was a symbol of that journey. A symbol of everything I'd learned, and everyone I'd met and learned with and from.

While this would be my last degree, the journey wasn't over. It was simply the start of a new journey of lifelong learning—just for the sake of it.

There would be no more papers, caps, or gowns. But there would always be more learning. And I could finally enjoy the learning process because there was nothing else to get.

On graduation day, I walked across the stage feeling at ease. The 50 words I wrote were narrated as I smiled at David, Joshua, Jacob, and the rest of my family from the stage.

> *I celebrate this journey as I begin another, but also bow to you in gratitude.*
>
> *Grateful for your confidence, love, and friendship. I'm hopeful.*
>
> *Hopeful that when history writes my story, it's a story of success.*
>
> *Success in my devotion to family, building community, and improving the lives of others.*

Truth and wisdom come from within, not from outside. Wisdom is about tapping into what we already know in ways that align deeply with our values.

This third section of the book focuses on expanding your understanding and awareness of what lies within. In this section, you'll learn how to notice, name, and decipher your own bodily sensations, and understand there's strong intellect in the emotions we feel.

By understanding your design, and how you make decisions as a human, you can replace bad habits and negative mental patterns with something better.

To make wise decisions, we need to go beyond logic. We need to be smarter than our thinking.

At the end of this section, my hope is that:

- you'll be able to respond more skillfully in the moment
- your awareness will be more finely tuned and developed
- you can see infinite opportunities in front of you.

You're smarter than your thinking

Logic is information. But information is only one part of understanding. To make wise decisions, we need to go beyond logic. We need to be smarter than our thinking.

When you put your car key in the ignition and turn it, the car starts. It just works.

But what happens when you turn the key and the car *doesn't start?*

You open the hood and look inside, right?

The same goes for being human. When something isn't working, we need to check under our hood. We need to turn inward, because getting better begins from within.

Look beyond the bounds of logic by reaching through the confusion and fear into your wisdom. Replace the limits that logic sets for us, and those we set for ourselves, with a world of possibility.

Throughout my life, I've accessed my wisdom and accepted the invitation to change (often through gritted teeth) by:

- facing the facts, but allowing life to lead me forward
- following my own truth instead of the "truth" of a book or cultural conditioning
- actively forging my own path
- letting go of piles of information to justify my decisions
- letting go of the need to find the logically "correct" answer[1]
- letting go of the limits logic puts on me, and replacing them with possibility.

Logic comes from the head. Happiness comes when we're in harmony with:

- our head (intellect)
- our heart (wisdom)
- our gut (instinct and intuition).

Or, to put it another way, when we've learned to Love Being Human.

---

[1] *I now realize there's no single "right" answer. There's only what's "right" for me right now.*

When we're out of alignment, our head, heart, and gut all try to pull us in different directions. When we follow only our head we're unbalanced, and something feels off.

The goal here is "alignment"–having our head, heart, and gut all pointing in the same direction so we can move forward confidently and smoothly.

Instead of letting outside forces such as logic pull you, start setting your own direction.

When logic argues for something negative, it's often lying. You can't make things go right by focusing on what could go wrong.

When your life is driven by logic, the logical conclusion is unhappiness.

These days I hold my vision in one hand and faith in the other.

Logic is a tool. But it's only one part of the equation. I've learned to let my life unfold before me.

Have you ever stopped yourself from fulfilling a dream or wish because logic told you something could go wrong, or that it might not work?

What if you let it *unfold* and lead you forward rather than stopping your life from taking its natural course?

When we live a life based on what's probable instead of what's possible, we miss out on so much. The probable lies in the realm of failure and impossibility, while the possible lies in the realm of creativity, delight, surprise, and joy.

We all want to be "smart" and "right" and "good". But it often means we never get to be our whole selves.

Who are you beneath the chaos?

I grew up around tornadoes in Texas. One day in fifth or sixth grade, I was playing Pong[2] when it suddenly sounded like a train was coming right into our house. It was so loud and chaotic I could barely hear myself think.

My mom yelled for us to get to the bathroom and climb into the tub.

"Just stay there and wait until it passes," she said.

We were told we couldn't do anything. There was a tornado coming. But we wanted to play. It seemed like fun. We didn't understand why Mom was so worried.

After a few minutes everything went quiet. Mom let out a sigh of relief, and we followed suit. Then it became

---

2   The early Atari video game where you bounced a ball back and forth on a black and white screen.

noisy again. And then everything went quiet and stayed that way.

My mom later explained that the brief moment of stillness was when the eye of the tornado had reached us. I was fascinated by that. The outer layers of a tornado are chaotic and bring destruction. But its center is always still and calm.

Whenever my emotions start swirling out of control, I remember that tornado. Getting stuck on the edges of my emotions leads to destruction. But when I can find the center (or float above it) I can find stillness and peace, and respond calmly instead of lashing out.

You can't play outside in the middle of a storm. You need to either let the storm pass or get to the center where there's no chaos.

For years I was considered a calm person who'd occasionally erupt like a volcano. But while my explosions seemed to come out of nowhere, they'd actually been bubbling up for a while.

Suppressing an emotion is like stuffing an inflated beachball underwater. We put so much effort into keeping the ball down, and yet the moment we get distracted it pops up again and splashes everyone around us.

You'll never know
who you truly are
until you take a seat
in the still center of
your soul.

I always held my tongue in public, but would lash out at the people I loved in private. I didn't understand anything about my emotions. Most of the time I couldn't even tell whether I was hungry or tired.

When I started identifying my bodily sensations, I'd notice that I needed to pee.

Then I'd think, *How long have I been holding this in?*

I'd read all about emotions and spirituality. But it was like reading about swimming without ever getting in the water. The word "embodiment" kept coming up, but I had no idea what it meant.

Until I started living it.

As I write this, I'm looking out the window. I know what the wind would feel like on my cheek. I can smell my garden, even though I'm inside. It all sounds so ordinary, but it's a level of experiential awareness I never had before.

And it means everything.

If you're always getting caught up in emotional tornadoes, you'll never know who you truly are until you take a seat in the still center of your soul.

Let's take the first step in that direction. (Allow three to five minutes for this experience.)

Exercise: A deeper presence

Start by uncrossing your arms and legs. Be attentive to the space around you, and take note of any sounds, smells, or bodily sensations you notice.

Now start to focus.

Draw your attention inward.

Press your lips together.

Breathe in through your nose.

How you get into a deeper presence or a neutral space will be unique to you. But here's a sequence that may help you get there.

Imagine your body is anchored to the earth.

Take note of your breath, your sensations, and your experience.

Slow yourself down so you can be present in this neutral flow of energy.

Take note of your feelings here. What are your sensations? What is your experience?

Take a few deep breaths, and then ask yourself:

> *How can I appreciate the love and guidance within me even more?*

Don't expect an answer to arise. Just let the question draw your attention as you move through your day. As you move through your week. As you settle into the evening. And even as you dream.

Let the curiosity of where you might find those answers draw you forward.

> *How can I appreciate the love and guidance within me even more?*

Take a few deep breaths.

Remember that all the tools you need are already within you. This isn't a skill you're learning for the first time. It's one you're rediscovering.

Understanding yourself better

Our brain is a problem-solving machine. It's not designed to sit in fulfillment or prioritize meaning.

If you let your brain become a racecar that takes you through life, you'll never slow down enough to enjoy the scenery. If you don't know how to apply the brakes in your brain, it can be a dangerous ride.

For example, during the "Dark Night of my Soul" I felt nonstop self-criticism.

I kept telling myself, *I'm smart. Why can't I get this right?* and *I'm trying so hard. Why can't I do it?*

I now know that our "operating system" is located in the most primitive part of our brain—the limbic system, where our "fight-or-flight" response resides.

We're hardwired to minimize danger. We're designed to move away from what we fear.

Dr. Evian Gordon, a neuroscientist at the University of Sydney Medical School, calls it the 1-2-4 brain model:

1. Our brain follows a key organizing principle: Minimize danger and maximize reward. The brain decides whether a situation is safe or threatening. When our brain decides a moment is threatening, our perception of reality is affected because we have five times as many neural networks for processing threats as we do for processing rewards.

2. Our brain has two operational modes: Conscious and non-conscious. Most of its operations function at the level of the non-conscious.

4. Our brain has four highly integrated ways to process information: Emotion, thinking, feeling, and self-regulation.

Your brain is designed to be afraid. It's designed to minimize your danger. So even if you don't recognize it and aren't consciously aware of it, you're designed for fear.

When I started pivoting away from what I was afraid of and toward what brought me joy, it created a significant shift in my life. Nothing was different on the outside, but everything got better on the inside. The war within came to a standstill. It's as if I established a peace agreement and created a psychological Switzerland within me.

I still knew why I was afraid. But moving toward what brought me joy was more important because I knew the fear wasn't a clear and present danger. In fact, it was more of a paper tiger.

When you focus your attention on any aspect of your experience, you embed or create neural pathways in your brain.

I've already mentioned my metaphor for the brain—a three-pound piece of tofu with a Dyson vacuum cleaner on top of it, and a spotlight mounted on top of that. Well, that spotlight is your attention. And your brain determines your experience based on whatever you point it at.

When I was wallowing in sorrow for all those years, I didn't know it was something I could control. I had no

There is no way to "fix" your design because there's nothing "wrong" with you.

idea I could train this "negativity bias" out of my brain. I just thought I was built wrong, or that something was wrong with me.

But when I started learning about the actual science of how human beings are designed, it gave me room to show compassion to both myself and other people.

There is no way to "fix" your design because there's nothing "wrong" with you. The work here is understanding what you need for yourself.

And that's tough. It's one of the things I still work through continuously.

For years, you've been served by that delightful brain you have. Its logic and reasoning have led you to where you are now. But now you're craving a deeper experience–something more fulfilling. It can't be given to you from the outside, nor can it be drawn out of another person. You literally need to generate it from within.

Understanding your brain:

- lets you understand your experience
- gives you more choices
- makes you more compassionate toward yourself and others.

Exercise: Perspective building

Imagine yourself looking at a painting that's stuck to the tip of your nose. You can't see the entire picture, can you?

Acknowledging you need to shift your perspective lets you step back from that inner war and get a good look at things.

Exercise: Mastering interoception

To free yourself from your automatic, unconscious responses you need to master a basic skill called "interoception".

Kirk Warren Brown, a professor at Virginia Commonwealth University, found a correlation between our level of interoception and our happiness. The more aware you are of your inner world, the happier and healthier you are, and the faster you heal from disease.

Interoception will help you step back from the war within.

Here's a quiz that will help you discover a baseline as you cultivate this core skill.

The Mindful Attention Awareness Scale (MAAS) is a 15-item scale designed to assess open or receptive awareness of, and attention to, what's currently taking place. (Here's where you can assess yourself: **bit.ly/lbh-maas**.)

Once you've assessed yourself, look at the numbers you selected. If they're at the 4/5/6 end of the scale, you're more disposed to mindfulness. And if they're at the 1/2/3 end of the scale, you're less disposed to mindfulness.

Developing the interoception skill gives us a good sense of our internal state. When we notice the subtle signals in our bodies, we can expand into more choices than what's available when we get caught up in emotion.

And it's in those choices that we find the magic.

We can't rely on our brain because it's interested only in keeping us away from danger. But when we bring our heart and gut into the mix, we have our entire nervous system helping us make decisions.

Exercise: Labeling emotions

As a young girl, I was taught to keep my emotions to myself.[3]

But when you suppress your emotions and don't talk about how you're feeling, your limbic (protection)

---

[3] *I still have no idea why, although it may have been a cultural thing. (I was Mexican and Catholic.)*

system either stays the same or gets worse. And when your limbic system is in high gear, it makes you less smart—it takes energy from your "thinking brain."

And here's where it gets *really* interesting.

You might think that by suppressing your emotions you're protecting yourself and those around you. But the truth is it can actually *increase* other people's blood pressure. They pick up on the emotions you're suppressing, and start perceiving you as a threat.

This was an earth-shaking revelation for me. By suppressing my emotions I was actually creating a threat response in the people around me.

So what changes did I make? I stopped suppressing my emotions, and started recognizing and labeling them instead. And that in turn allowed me to communicate better with others about how I was feeling.

I invite you to do the same.

Start by labeling your own emotions as they come up. The more you do this, the more your emotional vocabulary will widen, and the better you'll get at showing empathy and taking perspective.

You'll then become better at sharing your feelings in a simple way.

A good tool to help you build the vocabulary of your emotions is the Ekman's *Atlas of Emotions* (you can find it online) developed in conjunction with the Dalai Lama.

This simple tool will help shine a flashlight on your inner world, and help you step out of the war within yourself.

Pema Chödrön talks about "the hook"–our tendency to close down (and not give ourselves enough space) when we get caught up in emotion. We get "all worked up"–hooked in that moment of tightening when we reach for relief.

The better we get at labeling our emotions and recognizing what's hooked us, the better we'll get at relaxing in that moment.

This will lower that threat response, increase your sense of certainty, and help you:

- think better
- make better choices
- relate more to other people.

Try to let your thoughts, emotions, and sensations come and go without pulling you in or affecting you more deeply.

Exercise: Awareness of the breath

It's normal for your mind to wander away from your breath. Your brain has a core rhythm that operates on a rhythmic cycle between "tasks" and "drifting thoughts". You can condition this rhythm slowly over time. But if you haven't practiced that kind of meditation for years then mind wandering is completely normal. So don't sweat it. You can't change it overnight, nor do you need to.

Don't let this core physiological process frustrate you. Just bring your attention back to the breath when you notice that it's wandered.

Practice distancing yourself from what you notice when your mind wanders. Try to let your thoughts, emotions, and sensations come and go without pulling you in or affecting you more deeply.

Exercise: The 90-second rule

When a person reacts to something in their environment, their body undergoes a 90-second chemical process. If they feel any emotional response beyond those 90 seconds, it's because they've chosen to stay in that emotional loop.

This means that for 90 seconds you can watch the process happening, feel it happening, and then watch it go away.

But if you still feel an emotional response (fear, anger, etc.) after 90 seconds, you need to figure out what thoughts are re-stimulating the circuitry that keeps replaying that physiological response.

Exercise: Center yourself

Be. Here. Now.

Uncross your arms and your legs. Be attentive to the space around you, and take note of any sounds, smells, or sensations you notice.

Now start to focus.

Press your lips together.

Breathe gently through your nose.

Feel yourself starting to relax.

Feel the tension in your body start to release.

Scan through your body and find a place that feels tense.

Imagine a bubble forming around that place. Then imagine that bubble floating away and popping.

Repeat this process for any other areas in your body where you're holding tension.

Relax into your breath.

Breathe in and out through your mouth.

When you start your journey to the space of awareness in the present, you put yourself in receiving mode.

Here's a sequence that may help you move into being present in a neutral awareness.

Imagine your body is anchored into the earth.

Now imagine there's an energy field all around your body. The body is anchored into the earth, and you have this bubble of energy around you.

From this space, feel somewhere in your body that wants to open up. It might be tingling, or you might be feeling a sensation as that space opens its connection to your spirit and your soul.

Take note of your breath.

Take note of the sensation.

Notice yourself slowing down and being present in the natural flow.

Take note of the quality of your feelings.

What are your sensations like?

What's your experience like?

If thoughts are coming in, that's totally normal. Thank them for being there, and then come back to the present.

Come back to your connection to the source.

Take note of the quality of the experience. Understand the feelings coming up for you.

Take a couple of deep breaths here.

Now ask yourself:

> How can I appreciate the love and guidance within me even more?

Take some deep breaths while you ponder this question. Take as many as you need.

We can all change and be different.

Sit gently with that thought for as long as you need.

Exercise: Engage with creativity

I'd like you to consider or uncover a way you enjoy being creative. Something that engages your heart and your hands in a way that's genuinely yours.

I've been known to:

- fingerpaint
- play with clay to make mud pies

- play a game called jacks
- doodle and color.

Dancing, napping, and walking in the grass also count as a creative practice.

Choose your favorite form of creativity, and then take note of your feelings as you're being creative. Stay connected to your own experience.

Slow down, and be present in your own flow.

Journey to joy

If you've ever had a video call with me, you probably noticed my hair kind of "goes up" in a couple of places. Well, when I was seven I wore two barrettes in those spots. And even though I haven't worn barrettes in years, my hair still remembers those pins.

It's the same with my teeth. I went through Invisalign a year or two ago, and if I don't wear my retainer my teeth move back to where they used to be.

Your body remembers how things were. And when you're asleep at the wheel, it will "default" to how things used to be.

Unfortunately, the human "default" is to look at what's wrong, what isn't working, and what needs to be fixed.

When it comes to happiness, there's no set point for you. You can train yourself to be happier.

It's just the way we've been wired through thousands of years of evolution. Our brains are made of Teflon when it comes to happiness, and Velcro when it comes to what pisses us off, makes us sad, and makes us mad.

We can't always change our tendency to focus on the "lack" in our lives. But we *can* train ourselves to pay more attention to the things that bring us joy.

Science says we change through practice over time, or "drip by drip" as my favorite neuropsychologist Dr. Rick Hansen says.

Drip by drip, the things you pay attention to change the things you notice. And the things you notice open you up to more opportunities.

When it comes to happiness, there's no set point for you. You can train yourself to be happier.

My basic rules for this are to:

- keep it simple
- focus on the joyful
- commit to doing it for a specific period.

Your habits and rituals are deeply carved routes. And it will take a major effort to change them.

But if you're feeling stuck or in a rut, and want to level up your life experience, you *can* learn to think differently.

Change involves making connections, reinforcing new patterns, and building constructive habits.

You can choose to take a journey toward your joy.

Here are some exercises to help you.

Exercise: Notice the joy

Grab a notebook and a pen, set aside five minutes, and ask yourself this simple question: *What brought me joy today?*

If you're having trouble tuning in to joy, use these prompts as triggers:

- Did something make you happy?
- Did you experience wonder?
- Did something trigger your curiosity?
- Did someone do you a small kindness?

Want to take things slightly further? Ask yourself these questions:

- Why did it make me happy?
- Why did it create wonder for me?
- Why did it trigger my curiosity?
- Why did that small kindness make such an impression on me?

Exercise: Move toward joy rather than away from fear

During the "Dark Night of my Soul", I spent most of my time and energy focusing on:

- what I didn't want in my life and my relationships
- what I wouldn't accept
- what I didn't want to deal with.

As you can see, I was acutely aware of everything I didn't want.

What I *wasn't* thinking about were my own desires and what brought me joy.

But then I started focusing on what I *did* want rather than what I *didn't* want. I started moving away from what I feared and toward what I loved.

And things changed significantly.

So how do we do this?

Level One is to ask yourself these questions.

- What do I want here?
- What do I want now?
- What do I want from this?

If you're frustrated because you're not getting the answer, your answers keep changing, or you can't clear the obstacle between you and that clarity of your wanting, go easy on yourself. It's okay.

Level Two expands the level of inquiry.

- What choices do I have?
- How should I respond?
- What's here for me?

This level reminds me of when I'm looking for something to eat in the refrigerator. I'm asking myself what I want, but limiting myself to the choices I see in front of me.

Level Three is where you take generative action.

I once attended a training course at Zig Ziglar's worldwide headquarters in Dallas. During the course he talked about persistence, using a well as an analogy.

You've pumped it, and pumped it, and pumped it. But now you're sick of pumping the damn well, and you think, *It's dry. There's no water in that well.*

But Zig noted that if you keep pumping after the point where you're about to give up, that's when the water will probably start flowing.

And that's what consistent action is all about.

It might make you tired. It might hurt. It might even get you to the point where you think, *I don't think it's going to happen*. But you keep doing it, even if you can't see what's coming. Because pumping the well will bring the water up eventually. You just don't know how many pumps it will take.

While you should always acknowledge the level you're on right now, you also need to understand that level can change depending on:

- what you're asking
- what part of your life you're asking it from.

And that's okay. Just be aware, and let that awareness unfold. Give yourself time, and remember to keep gently shifting your focus to what you *do* want.

I have this picture of a circle. At the top of the circle is:

- what I don't want
- what I think I "should" do
- what I want that's best for everyone else
- what I want that's "right"
- what I want that's "safe".

At the bottom of the circle is what I want to do.

That resistance is something you need to accept.

I think of that circle as a rubber band. And between the top and bottom, between what I "should" do and what I *want* to do, is tension and resistance.

That resistance is something you need to accept. When you're moving from "what I should do", to "what I want to do", you're creating tension in the rubber band. It will pull on you every time you ask yourself, *Do I move forward or not?*

And it's strong. Very strong.

It's why you feel relaxed when you let that rubber band bring you back to where you feel "safe" again.

We need to retrain ourselves in what Seth Godin calls "buzzer management".

Think of a game show. As Seth points out, most contestants go for the buzzer before they know the answer. Why? Well, it's obviously a key part of the game. But they also do it because they believe the answer will come to them.

So how can you bring this approach to moving toward joy? How do you access Level One?

One exercise is to commit to journaling for 10 days using a single prompt: "What do I want?"

Ask yourself this same question every day for 10 days.

Write down whatever comes to mind. See what happens. See what pops up.

The second exercise comes from *Women Who Run With the Wolves* by Clarissa Pinkola Estés.

Take a piece of paper and draw a line down the middle. At the top of the left-hand column write "I must". And at the top of the right-hand column write "I must not".

Then fill the entire page.

>My parents say I must _____
>
>Society says I must _____
>
>My horoscope says I must _____
>
>My husband says I must not _____

What are the "musts" and "must nots"? What are the "shoulds"? Just bring your awareness to it.

I remember when my oldest son Joshua was coming home to visit, and I started making homemade enchiladas.

I hate cooking, so it was a ridiculous idea. But the way I was raised is deeply ingrained in me. Some of the best memories I have are of walking into my grandmother's house, and her immediately cooking something for me without even asking if I was hungry. I associated cooking with love, and so when I heard Joshua was coming home my immediate reaction was to make enchiladas.

My husband, David knew it was trouble, and so he wisely stayed out of the way. And sure enough, after 20 minutes I was cussing and frustrated.

But by the end of it I was laughing because I realized what was happening. "Oh, I'm doing this because I want to show him love. But this isn't how I show love. It's how my *grandmother* showed *me* love."

So, who's telling you what you should and shouldn't do? What are the "should dos" and "shouldn't dos"? Write them all down in the two columns.

You'll probably find this easier than the first exercise. It's always easier to focus on our "nos" and our "nots".

Exercise: Generating joy

Take both hands, and stroke them in a circular motion toward your heart.

If you feel more comfortable, hold yourself in the heart space with your dominant hand over your heart.

What feels more comfortable for you?

As you're making circular strokes around your heart, think of someone that brings you joy. Someone who's in your life now, or who was in it previously.

Go naturally at your own pace and rhythm, and take note of how the connection feels between your body and your hands.

As you bring that person to mind, notice what happens to your body. Be there for a little bit.

Enjoy this as a way of being present both individually and with each other.

Your body knows

A couple of years after my personal retreat from the world, I wanted a more structured escape. So I went on a ten-day, silent Vipassana meditation retreat.

My son Jacob was a senior at Aledo High School at the time, and so the first few days were rough.

But by day five or so I felt like I was breaking through. I finally believed I'd make it to the end.

Then I remembered Jacob's football team was in the state semifinals. Texas is famous for *Friday Night Lights*, and Aledo High School football is no joke. The show *Titletown, TX* follows the school's program, which has won the most state titles in Texas football history.

Missing this semifinal game would be a huge deal. What

if they lost and I never saw him play again?

At the retreat, I decided to use a tool I learned from Martha Beck (and have used with many clients) called The Body Compass. It's a way you can connect with your internal world to find out what's right for you and your truth.

Start by calibrating your body and figuring out what a "Yes" feels like compared to a "No".

1. Stand barefoot on the ground.
2. Think of a negative experience you can imagine comfortably. (I always imagine having to clean the family bathroom when my sons were teenagers.)
3. Take note of what it feels like. (For me it's like leaning backwards. But for you it might be like leaning forwards.)
4. Now think of a Million Dollar Moment – something that brings you deep joy.
5. Take note of what *that* feels like.
6. Remember the difference between the two. Do it as often as you need to calibrate your body.

Now, ask yourself a "Yes" or "No" question.

Our soul knows where we need to go. As long as we tune into what it's telling us, we can't possibly make a mistake.

I asked myself, *Should I leave the retreat and go to Jacob's game?*

My body immediately said "No", which seemed strange. How could my body not want me to support my son? I tried again. The answer was still "No". I kept fighting it, repeating the test six or seven times because I couldn't believe what my body was telling me.

But the answer was always "No".

It had taken guts (and a year of planning) to make it to that retreat. It was incredibly important to me, and I wasn't sure I'd ever have two free weeks to meditate again.

Jacob's team won the semifinals, and the following week I watched them win the championship.

If I'd left the retreat without completing it, I would have regretted it forever.

My head was convinced I needed to leave. But my body knew better. Going to Jacob's game was important, but making time for myself was even more important.

It would have been tough if it was Jacob's last game and I missed it. But it was just a story. It wouldn't have made me selfish to do what my soul needed.

The hardest decisions are those that are closest to us. But our soul knows where we need to go. As long as we tune in to what it's telling us, we can't possibly make a mistake.

You can't do this alone

Humans are social beings. I learned from my research that whenever you try to be "different" and pull yourself away from your social structure, it's going to be painful.

Social pain lights up the same areas of your brain as physical pain. If someone turns away from you, rolls their eyes, or just disses you, it will put you into what some call an *amygdala hijack* (a very fearful state). Research shows that numbing physical pain by taking Tylenol also numbs the parts of the brain that light up when you experience social pain.

Maslow's Hierarchy of Needs identifies safety, shelter, and food as basics we need to meet before we can attend to the higher needs of love and belonging.

But research by neuroscientist Matthew Lieberman suggests our need to connect with other people is even more fundamental than our need for food or shelter.

I'm emphasizing this because as you transform into a new way of being, you must be connected to at least one human who can support you.

If your immediate social circle doesn't support your shift, then chances are you'll revert back to your baseline. Your brain won't let you grow out of those relationships because it believes it's more important for you to *belong* than to *learn and grow* into that deeper sense of self you want to connect to.

I inched toward something different for almost seven years. But the metamorphosis didn't start until:

- my boys became men
- I became an "empty nester"
- my husband retired from the military.

This led to a significant shift in my identity. I didn't recognize my world anymore. It felt like the walls were collapsing around me. I lost all my social networks and avenues for connection at once.

And it was tough.

That's why it is critical to have someone who can support you through your transformation.

If you're processing trauma, you might have a therapist. If you want to achieve an outcome, you might have a coach. Most of my clients have a full array of support. They typically have an entire team to support their desired change, including nutritionists and physical trainers.

I firmly believe that what makes them successful is that they know how to reach out beyond their immediate loved ones for help.

It's not easy for a person to look at someone they're close to and say, "It's okay for you to change." We recognize that evolution is necessary up to our teenage years. But once we've matured we're not as compassionate toward shifts, and people typically like to be comfortable and want things to stay the same.

The journey to self

Being human is an acceptance of, and compassion for, our fundamental biological impulses and reflexes.

Want to know what I think separates people from themselves and each other, and makes them feel confused, disillusioned, and without meaning? It's when they walk into a building or an office, and feel they need to be somebody different from who they actually are.

There's this concept of living the "right" way. I've certainly been someone who has tried to live the "right" way–from the expectations of my parents, my education, and my facilitators right through to everything on the big grand cultural spectrum.

But doing things the "right" way didn't get me what I wanted, or where I wanted to be.

So I had to make changes. I had to adjust my mindset.

How?

In the end, what worked best for me was constant reminders–looking within and giving myself space to realize what was right for me instead of the external factors.

So many people in the later stages of their lives say, "I always did something for someone else. I never did it for myself." And it reminds me of this quote by Carl Jung:

> Your vision will become clear only when you can look into your own heart. Who looks outside, dreams; who looks inside, awakens.

This was certainly my experience. But it took decades to figure it out, because I believed that if I did the "right" things in the "right" way I'd get what I wanted.

Do this, get that.

But then I found myself living the American dream and not being able to enjoy it. It brought tremendous guilt. But it also unlocked the place I am today–a place where I can derive joy from the simplicity of daily life. A place where I can help people find that same joy.

I love reminding people that no matter how big or small your life is, you can access the same level of meaning and joy as everyone else. It doesn't matter how many shoes you have in your closet, how many outfits you own, or

Being human is
an acceptance of,
and compassion for,
our fundamental
biological impulses
and reflexes.

how many cool people you know. You'll always have access to that internal wellspring of joy and meaning.

So many people with these outward things don't know how to fill that meaning up. And that's what happened to me. I had everything—all the trappings of success. And then I looked at myself and said, "What the heck? When do I get to be happy?", as if happiness was an object.

Things changed significantly when I turned inward and started exploring my sense of self.

When I reflect on those "Dark Years" I can see it's where my "self" was dying. The "self" who was the mother. The "self" who was the military spouse. The "self" who was a volunteer and leader in the community.

The thought that this person would no longer exist was painful.

But once I let that person go into the wild west of yesteryear, it freed the human I am now. And this human is so much more beautiful. Whenever I see someone, they immediately see the difference in me.

Maybe it's just semantics. But rather than battling the idea of one self versus many selves, perhaps it's easier to talk about layers of the ego versus your self.

This makes it easier to let your current self go so your true self can emerge.

But as I said earlier, it's not easy. We'll resist it simply because we don't know any better.

When you're suffering—on the floor, or in a corner sort of crumpled up into a ball—that's a posture of resistance.

It could be simple, but instead we make it complicated.

Still, that's the fun part, isn't it? After all, it's kind of a game.

It tingles when we're on the brink—battling between transformation and resistance.

For me, it's a different spin on an old story. In the past I helped people with tools and careers. Now I help people with vocations and purpose. It's as if my previous vocation was learning how to go into that deeper essence the soul desires. As if it all led to this.

In the past, I was dominated by fear. I made decisions based on what I feared.

The difference now is that instead of moving away from fear, I move toward love. When I lay my head down at night I say my prayers, and give my thanks. And I'm grateful for everything while looking at where I could have been better.

And when I open my eyes in the morning I'm so surprised and feel so blessed that I get to do it all again.

It's so different from the life I led before. I was always rushing, never getting enough sleep, and never having enough time or enough of anything.

I now have far more than I know what to do with.

On the outside, nothing has changed. The only thing that's different is the way I make meaning out of my life from inside to out.

Humans are meaning makers.

Shifting from a mindset of checking lists to one of creating movements from one thing to another is like comparing a ladder to a symphony of music and individual notes that come together to become a song.

You're not climbing a boring ladder where you reach the top only to find there's nothing to see up there.

Instead, you're making music. You're creating a symphony with every step you take.

Within and between, within ourselves and between each other. That's all life is. It's the meaning we make, and the relationships and experiences we share.

It's important to remember that the journey to self is just that: A journey. There are many different paths, loopholes, and other things you could go through on the way. And with each step you can look back to what it was like before, and see things from the other side. Nine times out of ten, once you're on the other side you'll never want to go back.

It's not that you *can't* go back to where you came from—back to your tribe or your old people. It's just that you can't unsee what you've already seen.

Your sense of self is like a seed. You're nurturing it, giving it space, and giving it water. But you're not doing the growing. You're *allowing* it to grow.

And what you're allowing to grow is your way—your true nature.

FINAL REFLECTION: HUMAN

Life is your teacher, experience is your classroom, and learning means remembering. When we understand how we're wired, we can transform ourselves. We no longer struggle to move forward, and our journey toward lasting change becomes easier and easier.

Conclusion

The *Love Being Human* method is built on a foundation of understanding how we're wired as human beings. It allows our inner knowing to emerge. It puts our feet on a path that's grounded in self-compassion. It's a process that opens your heart, magnifies your spirit, and changes your mind.

Remember: The divine discontent you feel signals your growth, and pulls you forward.

- Walk toward your joy instead of moving away from what you fear.
- Defy logic, use the MINE process for setting goals, and open yourself to what's possible instead of just what's probable.

Allow your identity to evolve — we're constantly changing and learning.

- Let go of your "shoulds", and be more open and playful.
- Let your values guide you, not the expectations of others.

Remember that deeper connections start by becoming intimate with yourself. Allow your identity to evolve—we're constantly changing and learning.

Remember that your consciousness filters stimuli. Set an intention for what you want so you can see it come to life. Facts matter far less than people think.

Remember that a pause or a step backward isn't failure. It's simply part of the dance. The Texas Two-Step is a reminder that one step forward and two steps back is a natural rhythm.

I hope this book has taught you to:

- understand how your brain and body are wired (and how to retrain it)
- develop a kind, gentle approach to daily practice
- distinguish the difference between belonging and trying to fit in
- nurture yourself with kindness and self-compassion, as it's the only way to coax your soul into a deeper unfolding

- heal with compassion and community
- stop focusing on happiness. It's a fleeting feeling. Forge your path to joy and unshakable peace instead.

The most important thing now is to take action.

The insight will follow.

Thank you for letting me be part of your journey.

Acknowledgments

Thank you to everyone who helped me with the writing and editing of various drafts of this book in its many stages, especially Kelly.

Thank you to everyone who read early versions of this book, including Julie, who poured both hours and love into her gentle feedback.

Thank you to my Patreon supporters over the years, including Henry, Sarah, and Ronnie. Your support has fueled my creativity.

Thank you to the Within (U)niversity members. Over the last decade, we've explored our way through countless spiritual quests. We tuned in completely and listened deeply, and it was our soul food. Together we've practiced trusting our intuition on the journey to learning about ourselves—who we are, where we're at, and where we want to be. It's been my honor to walk alongside you on your sacred journey.

Thank you to all my friends and family who have helped me make this philosophy a lived reality.

Thank you, Christine Sperber, my former mentor and now a treasured friend. Te adoro.

Thank you to the communities of practice that have supported my growth over the last decade. They include Martha Beck's March 2015 Wayfinder Life Coach Training Cohort, Martha Beck's Wayfinder Master Coach Training 2016 cohort, Modern Elder Alumni and Comadres from the July 2019 Dancing Brujas cohort, my fellow Remarkables in Seth Godin's Forward Link Alumni community, the Finders Community Inner Circle, Wisdom 2.0's 2021 The Heart's Path Community, CreativeMornings Global Community of Hosts and Volunteers, altMBA 37 alumni, A Mighty Kindness House of Belonging community, Andy Ward's Ancient Pottery community, and Beverly Belling's Intuitive Arts Studio Community.

About the Author

Dr. Vivian Hernandez Carrasco is a wife and mother of grown men. She is a modern mystic, mentor, and spiritual companion who has helped hundreds of tender hearts and kind souls make lasting personal transformations.

Vivi is the founder of Within (U)niversity, a learning community of mindful leaders, creatives, and seekers forging their personal spiritual path. She is the host of the podcast, Within (U) with Dr. Vivian Carrasco.

Her recent projects include being the co-founder and former host of the CreativeMornings Fort Worth chapter from 2019 to 2022. She is currently the CEO of Fort Worth Creative Collaborations, a non-profit organization.

As an academic, Vivi conducted her doctoral research on collaboration.

As an organizational consultant, her past professional life revolved around reaching far and wide to develop partnerships. From local, community-based relationships to national friendships, she knows firsthand about the meaning and fulfillment that can be found in connecting with others.

Vivi's work in the world is focused on helping make change easier; she believes better begins within.

Learn more at **viviancarrasco.com** and **withinuniversity.com**

www.ingramcontent.com/pod-product-compliance
Lightning Source LLC
Chambersburg PA
CBHW071003160426
43193CB00012B/1903